Tastes *of* Britain

Dorinda Hafner was born in Ghana and came to the UK to train as an opthalmic nurse and dispensing optician. Although she accomplished this aim, Dorinda's love of dance and performance led to a career in the performing arts. She moved to Australia with her husband and two children and, for the past 21 years, has worked as story-teller, actress, dancer, choreographer, public speaker, writer and television cook. Her many television appearances there have made her a greatly loved personality for her warmth and humour.

Dorinda's food anthropology programmes and their companion books, *A Taste of Africa*, *A Taste of the Caribbean* and *United Taste of America*, have been hugely successful on Channel 4 and in the US, Canada, Australia and many other parts of the world. Dorinda divides her time between the UK and Australia.

Tastes *of* Britain

Dorinda Hafner

Kyle Cathie Limited

To James and Nuala, for your rich heritage

Special thanks to:
Channel 4 for the continuing opportunity to share fun and meaningful food programmes with our many viewers, and to Richard Hurst and Andrew Brann, Ros Franey (executive producer), directors Cassie Farrell (producer/director), David Presswell, Mark Strickson and Patricia Murphy – for your diversity and vision.
Tom Archer (Factual & Development, HTV West), Bill Meehan (line producer) and to HTV itself – thanks for the series
Susan Hicks – for her help in developing and testing the recipes

The Contributors:
Greek – Mary Spyrou, Mahi Theo, Michael & Goula Economou & family, Anna & Ronnie Melemeni & family, the Annastasi family, Mr Phillipos & wife, Mary & Janis at Helepi
Irish – Regina Sexton, Sinéad ní Shuinéar, Sue Hicks
Afro-Caribbean – Delroy, Loletta & Angela Rolle, Pauline Findlayson & Paulette Dixon, Mr & Mrs Albert Stewart, Natasha Clarke, Cass (Mr Hot Doubles), Kantiba, Abeje, Hadiya, Sophie, Abiba, Obi, Siobhon, Ashley and all at the Kuumba Project in St Paul's, Bristol
Pakistani – Mohamed Aslam, Mumtaz Khan Akbar, Mr & Mrs Abbas & family, Leeb Akhtar, Yasmin Ansari,
Scottish – Ackergill Castle – Simon MacDonald, Craig Rowland, Lisa, Eric, Frannie & Jeannie 'Carroy' Farquhar & family, Tom & Angela Mackay, Mr & Mrs Alan Joyce, Stewart Wishart, Charlie Stewart & Billie Stewart
Italian – Giovanni Malacrino
Jewish – Claudia Roden, Aviva & Moshe Ellis, Oded Schwartz, Sue & Kenny at Café on the Green and Jay Rayner
English – Hattie Ellis, Sue Hicks
Chinese – Dennis Ford, Harry Kui Shum Yeung, Wing-Shing Chu (Yang Sing restaurant), Yung Yung Wah, John & Linda Lee (New Emperor restaurant), James Ho (Ho's Bakery), Kin Man Lee (Oriental Express), Lauren X.B. Lee & family, Kim Chan, So Kwan, Kok Cheong Tang & Tian Guan Buddhist Temple, Master Chu, Dr Chee

Thanks also to:
Julia Scott – for your energy, wonderful and zany ideas for publicity
Lois Allender – the 'mife' we all want to have, namely that wonderful combination of mother and wife
Kyle Cathie – the first hands-on publisher I've worked with – you're great!
Sarah Harrison – as the envelope said to the stamp, stick with me and we'll go places
Mark Farrell – for seeing things through the Englishman's eye, a big thank you for your scribbles and thoughts
Stephanie Horner – thanks for pushing the boundaries of time and editing
Julie Dixon – what the eye does not see the heart does not grieve over, so where are the food shots you discarded?
Cassie Farrell – for your boundless energy and insatiable appetite for making fun documentary programmes
Olivia Oppong, my make-up artist – Olivia, thanks for putting my best face on for the cover and cameras
Hattie Ellis, researcher – for your stupendous knowledge
Alison Thomas, researcher – for your enthusiasm and foot miles
Rob Mitchell, researcher – I hope we managed to fill you with a 'tad' of sauciness as well as colour to your cheeks!
Dewi Gregory, researcher – for finding the best *gelati* in Wales
Lisa Upton, production secretary – for keeping the connections going when all else went mad
Michael Ladkin, my agent – let's hope you continue to help the 'dough' rise
Angela Miller – it takes many scribbles to make one wisdom, so I'll keep writing, thanks
Mary Clemmey – thank you for pulling the cat out of the bag

First published in Great Britain in 1998 by
Kyle Cathie Limited
20 Vauxhall Bridge Road
London SW1V 2SA

ISBN 1 85626 307 X

Text copyright © 1998 by Dorinda Hafner
Photographs copyright © 1998 by Julie Dixon

Book design by Geoff Hayes
Production by Lorraine Baird

Dorinda Hafner is hereby identified as the author of this work in accordance with Section 77 of the Copyright Designs and Patents Act 1988.

Printed in England by Butler and Tanner Limited, Frome

Photographic acknowledgements: All transparencies in the introductions by Mark Farrell, with the exceptions of pages 46, 47 and 96 – Cassie Farrell, and pages 62 and 63 – Alison Thomas

Contents

Introduction

'Dishes are important because they are a link with the past, a celebration of roots, a symbol of continuity. They are that part of an immigrant culture which survives the longest, kept up even when clothing, music, language and religious observance have been abandoned.'

CLAUDIA RODEN – *THE BOOK OF JEWISH FOOD*

What is British food? I live in Australia and I travel around the world learning about food and people – the origins of both and their interaction with each other. I get to hear a lot of opinions expressed about various foods. A recent publicity tour around the United States of America however, convinced me that, in the race for culinary supremacy, British food has had bad press. The very mention of British cuisine seems to be met with a grimace or a laugh of mockery. What is it about the cuisine which has this effect on people?

When people say British food desperately needs a facelift, surely they mean English food, not the collective term? As I see it, British food today is the glorious heritage of many nationalities.

I do not propose to know all the answers but I think the industrial revolution, the second world war and the advent of processed foods have all played a major role in tampering with earlier British tastes and cuisine. But the importation of foreign labour into Britain after the war, the arrival of Commonwealth citizens, the cross-cultural pollination that comes with international business affairs, the advent of air travel to foreign places for holidays and the arrival of refugees in recent years, combine to mean that British palates can now enjoy the sort of foreign fare which was once the prerogative of only the very rich. British cuisine has almost overnight become a rich tapestry of multicultural exotica.

Fish and chips is no longer the favourite of the nation – this has apparently changed to curry and probably will change again. But the interesting thing is that the next number one dish will probably be ethnic also. Yes, 'British food' is getting its facelift, so why hasn't the rest of the world woken up to this to give 'British food' a break?

Take a tour around the food of Britain, and you get a pretty good history lesson at the same time. The Saxons were here when the Normans arrived in 1066 with William the Conqueror, bringing with them culinary terms so that Britons could eat beef instead of cow, mutton instead of sheep and venison instead of deer; that respect for French cuisine has lasted a millennium. These Anglo-Saxon-Normans then embarked on hundreds of years of overseas adventures and conquest, starting on their doorstep with the Irish in the twelfth century, and progressively spreading out into the rest of the world. Eight hundred years later, when it was all over, there were some interesting mixes to be found – like Caribbean islands where Africans, Chinese, Indians and English lived together. And a fair cross-section of the old

empire was to be seen in Britain itself. Add various nationalities who have taken refuge from pogroms or from poverty – Italians, Poles, Russians, Jews, and later Ethiopians and Somalis – and you have today's particular list of population ingredients, plus a recipe for some very interesting food indeed.

You only need to walk down any high street of any British city and you see, often behind giant neon lights, Chinese, Italian, Greek or Indian restaurants. A certain testament to the changing face of British cuisine! But where is *the* British Eatery? This victual revolution is not restricted just to high streets and restaurants. In private homes people are trying out the myriad of cross-cultural fare on offer at the local supermarket, they are buying and cooking recipes from new cookbooks, they are doing fusion cooking – you name it, they are trying it. Cooking shows have proliferated on our television screens and we are loving them!

Food has developed legs. Food now country-hops as much as its consumers. Food is changing nationalities by the minute. People are eating 'foreign' more and more and fusion cooking is all the rage. A fascinating collection of different elements goes to make up the identity of an expatriate 'ethnic group'. Sometimes the most important is 'ethnicity' itself, sometimes language or religion. Then there's the vague term 'culture' – which includes traditions, family life, music, clothes, maybe sense of humour and, of course, food. There's nothing quite so evocative as the sight and smell of a dish that your granny made for you. So it's no surprise that people who wish to hold a community together, pay special attention to their distinctive cuisine.

Lots of tourists come to Britain to see history. They want grandiose palaces, immaculate guardsmen, antiques, pubs where Emily Brontë might have been in for a pint of stout. They expect fog, and maybe even steam trains. And they're not always disappointed. There are corners of Britain which have successfully turned themselves into heritage theme parks. You can visit the manor gardens, catch a bit of morris dancing and buy a jar of jam with a little cloth hat on it. But what the tourists are at first mystified by, and later delighted to discover, is that modern Britain tells a much richer and more complex story than that. It slowly dawns on them that the Africans, Sikhs, Chinese, Greeks, Jews and Italians on the bus are not tourists like themselves – these people live here. They have their shops, restaurants, clubs, churches, mosques and parts of town. Some are hanging on to distinct cultures, others are blending in bit by bit. But they're here, and they make a difference. The cloves of garlic may disappear in the tomato sauce when you turn the blender on, but you can still taste them all right! The Scots, Irish and Welsh are also part of the blend: not wearing kilts or shamrock or miners' lamps, but adding their special idiosyncratic flavours to the mix nevertheless.

I've seen a lot of changes in Britain since I lived here back in the mid-60s and early 70s. The restaurant scene is probably the most visible. Asian and Italian food was just taking off in those days. All the burger joints were Wimpy, and they only did takeaway if you asked them nicely. It was a tall order if you fancied Thai, Lebanese, Persian, Japanese or Moroccan. These days you can take your pick: you can have Greek or Turkish kebabs, Szechwan or Cantonese Chinese, North or South Indian, Indonesian, Korean, Caribbean, Afghani, Ethiopian, you name it. Just as prodigious has been the spread of ingredients to shops. In those far-off days not every food shop had long spaghetti. Sweet potatoes and mangoes were exotic treats involving a trip to Brixton market. Now they're on supermarket shelves all over the country, along with avocados, tiger prawns, fennel, basmati rice, couscous, squid, sesame oil, shiitake and porcini mushrooms, papaya, scotch bonnet chillies, ginger...

By a happy coincidence in the 60s, just as new immigrants settled in, bringing with them their excellent culinary traditions, the British decided to break a habit of a lifetime and start going out to restaurants. Or was it the supply that led to the demand? Whatever the truth behind this chicken-and-egg conundrum, the highly satisfactory result is that now the British restaurant scene is just buzzing. New eating places jostle for space in the high streets. The French and Italians may be (rightly) proud of their food, but you'll find more variety if you're dining out in Manchester than ever you will in Bordeaux or Bologna.

For years the British avoided eating 'foreign'; some even went as far as carrying their own food and beverage with them on holidays. That used to mean packing the cornflakes, white sliced bread and tins of corned beef, just in case you couldn't get anything edible overseas. But these days, as well as eating out, people have been returning home wanting to re-create new ethnic tastes in their kitchens or even re-visit these authentic tastes in the foreign restaurants in their locality. Suitcases have become lighter, although that's partly down to the fact that you can now get cornflakes on the Costa Brava! There's a nice Irish saying: 'Taste it and then you will desire it.' And yet there are still pockets of the hardy brigade who continue to apply the principle in reverse: 'I'm not trying it because I don't like it!'

Today people are being weaned off many of their old favourites. I haven't seen an advert for custard powder or gravy powder for ages. Salad cream is giving way to dressing, first in bottles and then home-made. Fish paste and that strange 'sandwich spread' are long obsolete. Lard and suet are battling for their market share. Tinned fruit and evaporated milk as dessert just don't seem necessary any more. Everybody in this country is more daring than they used to be. British tastebuds have never had it so good – in an unprecedented fashion, they're being challenged every which way with something exotic every day.

More than anywhere except perhaps the USA, cooks in Britain want to follow recipes in books – and long may they continue to do so, I say! Actually there's been something of a tradition of cookbooks in this country, from the seventeenth century onwards. In that early period of course society was organised in a very different way. The poor stuck to a limited range of well-tried dishes, and their library consisted of a bible. The better-off had cooks, and the lady of the house was too busy overseeing the whole operation and setting up the social diary to mess around a lot in the kitchen. So most of the cookbooks were either learned treatises, with historical and scientific references, or they were professional manuals for chefs. Those aimed at women were dilettante in tone, like *The Genteel House-Keeper's Pastime*, or *The Accomplisht Lady's Delight in Preserving, Physick, Beautifying and Cookery* (1677). The English realised that the French could teach them a thing or two, and there were some French cookbooks on the market. But, as the two countries were often at war, the English liked to pretend that their neighbours were despicable in every way, and their food was fussy and over-elaborate compared with good solid, wholesome roast meat with a mug of ale. I have a sneaking suspicion that some of that sort of prejudice has survived right up to the present day.

Mrs Beeton, and Eliza Acton before her, were thought of as the very essence of Englishness and, sure enough, editions of Beeton's immensely popular books are full of ideas for boiled beef, jellied eels and bread pudding. But even then, at the peak of Victorian self-confidence, the odd foreign or colonial idea crept in. There's Italian macaroni pie, American 'jombalayah', fricassee of kangaroo tail (you can guess where that's from) and Indian kedgeree. In the case of kedgeree, Mrs B gives an Indian and an adapted version: the former has dhal, ghee, ginger and cardamom, the latter became one of the most popular of a whole class of Anglicised recipes that didn't bear much of a resemblance to the exotic originals. In the end, almost anything with rice and fish (coloured yellow and often with a few leftovers thrown in) was called kedgeree. At least these hints of foreign ways showed the beginnings of an open mind.

In this cookbook I take a look at nine of the many different ethnic communities in Britain, and offer you a

selection of recipes, some of which are featured in my TV series. There are many more communities to enjoy and I hope this is just the start to a long and delicious journey into the future of cosmopolitan Britain. You may want to use the recipes as a springboard – have a go! Practise something different until you discover which of the many sumptuous flavours featured suit you, then sit down and enjoy with my blessing! Or you may prefer, as I often do, to skim through and just get inspiration for original ingredients, new combinations or different ways of preparing things. Have you ever flavoured your cakes with ground cherry stone kernel, called 'mechlepi' by the Greeks? It's a unique and mysterious scent and flavour. I bet you've made curries with lamb; why not give goat a try? I guarantee you'll enjoy it – and you'll earn a lot of praise for your enterprise. Perhaps you're a good cook, but stuck in rut. In that case, tackle some of those challenging Indian and Chinese dishes: they may take a while to prepare but the taste is magical, and let me assure you that they can be cooked without supernatural powers. Great oaks from little acorns certainly have grown.

Bon appetit.

Chapter 1: Afro-Caribbean

The first black people to come to the British Isles were a cosmopolitan army soldiers a couple of thousand years ago – that of the Romans. whose troops were recruited from every corner of their far-flung empire. Eventually the Romans lost their grip on their conquests and went home. Black people were not seen on these shores again until the 16th century. when British traders and the navy started to take a (rather unhealthy) interest in Africa.

The next 300 years brought black and white together in the worst possible relationship. Slavery was at the heart of the history of the period. It made America and the Caribbean what they are today. It made Britain rich and powerful and able to expand its empire around the globe. It gave Britain the capital to fund the industrial revolution.

The meeting of the old and new worlds changed the eating habits of the people on both sides for ever. One great boon for the Africans arriving in the Caribbean was that. with the familiar climate. they could continue to grow their favourite vegetables from home. They were also confronted with a cornucopia of new and surprising foods – cassava. sweet potatoes. maize. peanuts. guavas. pineapples. chillies. sugar cane and vanilla. The combination of tradition with discovery created an explosion of culinary invention. Add to this the contributions of the French. Spanish. Portuguese. British and Dutch. Then. a bit later. import some Chinese and Indians. Wow! Just about the whole world meets up in the loveliest imaginable rendez-vous… and that's the Caribbean for you.

Haili Campbell with fruit cocktail

Slavery was abolished in the British empire in 1834. But it wasn't until the 1950s and 60s that Afro-Caribbeans came to Britain in numbers: today there are about half a million people of Caribbean origin living in the UK.

But what about their cosmopolitan cuisine? Whilst every other ethnic group seems to specialise in the catering business. Afro-Caribbean eating houses are few and far between. There are street markets. yes. So people are taking home their yams. sweet potatoes and mangoes. their Scotch bonnets and ginger and saltfish. and no doubt concocting fabulous dishes – which they are not sharing with the rest of us! But you can't keep something this good down for ever. The past few years have seen a new pride and self-confidence amongst Afro-Caribbeans. Restaurants have started to appear in the USA and the same is now happening here. particularly in Brixton. Apart from anything else, young Afro-Caribbeans need to see that their ancestral diet is valued; too many of them live on pizzas, burgers and beans!

We're not just talking about Jamaican patties, rice 'n' peas and rum. We're talking about the most glorious raw materials – fabulous fish and vegetables, with loads of herbs and spices, and flavours like coconut milk and molasses. Then there are all the variations between the islands. Jamaica itself has masses to offer, from curried goat, through jerk pork to ackee and salt fish. Trinidad is big on Indian influence, with curries and 'roti' on every street corner. Martinique can boast a winning combination of classic French with tropical Creole cuisine. Barbados is the most British of islands, and yet there use lots of chilli and lime juice in their souse. Grenada, the world's greatest nutmeg producer, is called the 'Isle of Spice', so you can well imagine what distinguishes its particular blend of English and French cuisine. St Lucia seems to specialise in heavier stews full of African roots like yam, sweet potato and dashine.

Today there's good reason for their cuisine to catch on and this includes the Rastafarian cuisine with its philosophy of 'ital' food – absolutely pure ingredients with no pesticides or fertilisers or processing. In other words simple organic raw materials – and, at the beginning of the new millennium, isn't that what we are all looking for?

The cultural links – Africa meets Jamaica in Bristol.

Natasha's Red Peas Soup

Serves 6

250g (9oz) red kidney beans, soaked
  overnight
1.1–1.7 litres (2–3 pints) water
1–2 salted pig's tails, soaked
  overnight, cut into small pieces
  or 225g (8oz) salt pork, soaked
  overnight, diced small
1–2 tablespoons cornmeal

for the vegetables
prepare traditional West Indian
vegetables as available, to a total
weight of about 900g–1.4kg (2–3lb):

450g (1lb) yam), peeled and cubed
450g (1lb) dashine, peeled and cubed
1 breadfruit, not too ripe, peeled,
  seeds discarded and cubed
450g (1lb) sweet potato, cubed
450g (1lb) coco (callaloo) leaves
  (sometimes known in Jamaican
  markets as 'Bhaji', or substitute
  spinach or Swiss chard
1 medium onion, peeled and chopped
2 skellion, crushed (from West Indian
  shops), or spring onions
2 cloves garlic, peeled, crushed and
  roughly chopped

for the seasonings
3 sprigs of fresh thyme
1 teaspoon mixed dried herbs
generous pinch or two of Season-all
  powder (from West Indian shops)
salt and freshly ground black pepper
dash of West Indian hot pepper sauce

for the dumplings
225g (8oz) plain flour
1 tablespoon baking powder
good pinch of salt
25g (1oz) butter
chilled water to mix

for thickening the soup (optional)
25–50g (1–2oz) cornmeal

to finish
chopped fresh herbs, to your
preference and taste

This is a simple 'homely' soup, Natasha's equivalent to Scotch Broth or Irish stew in which root vegetables, meat and local green vegetables are combined and slowly cooked together. Depending on how you like your soup you can make it thinner or spicier as you please. In Natasha's original recipe, she advocates 'a generous pinch of Season-all powder', a commercial preparation from supermarkets. However, I substituted a combination of ½ teaspoon each of celery salt, onion salt, freshly ground black and white pepper and paprika without compromising on taste.

1 Begin preparation a day ahead by pre-soaking beans and salted meat. Put the pre-soaked beans and their soaking liquid into a large heavy-based pan, add 1.1–1.7 litres (2–3 pints) water and bring to the boil on a medium flame. Add the chopped pre-soaked pig's tails or pork. Skim the froth from the surface of the broth, turn the flame to low, partially cover the pan and simmer gently for 30 minutes, skimming from time to time if necessary, until the broth is clear.

2 Meanwhile, make the dumplings. Sift the flour, baking powder and salt into a mixing bowl. Rub in the butter with cold fingers and thumbs, use a knife to mix in enough chilled water to bind, and gather the mixture into a very stiff dough. Divide into about 15 portions, shape between your hands into balls, flatten into 'finger' dumplings and set aside.

3 Now add the prepared selection of vegetables to the soup. If necessary top up the soup with a little boiling water. Cover the pan and continue to simmer very gently for a further 15 minutes, gradually adding all the seasonings and flavouring ingredients, tasting and checking the flavours as the dish is cooking.

4 Drop the dumplings into the pan and continue simmering for a further 15–20 minutes. At this stage of the cooking, if necessary, stir in 1–2 tablespoons of cornmeal to thicken the soup slightly. The dish is ready when all the ingredients are tender and cooked right through.

5 Serve hot in warmed bowls. Sprinkle with chopped fresh herbs to taste and a dash of West Indian pepper sauce if you have it.

Cou-Cou and Flying Fish

Serves 6

for the Cou-cou
32 tender young okra
2.8 litres (5 pints) water
3 teaspoons salt
900g (2lb) fine yellow cornmeal, sifted
4 tablespoons butter

for the flying fish
6 flying fish
juice of 2 limes, 1 tablespoon reserved
   salted water
6 tablespoons sifted flour, mixed with
   ½ teaspoon mixed dried herbs
2 large onions, peeled and very finely
   hashed, half reserved for sauce
1 bunch of parsley, roughly chopped,
   half reserved for sauce
1 bunch of fresh thyme, leaves
   stripped and roughly chopped, half
   reserved for sauce
good pinch salt and a few turns of
   freshly ground pepper
vegetable oil for frying

for the sauce
2 tablespoons vegetable oil and 2
   tablespoons butter for frying
reserved onion, finely hashed
reserved parsley and thyme, roughly
   chopped
6 tomatoes, peeled and chopped, and
   their juices
150ml (¼ pint) water

to finish
lots of wedges of lime or lemon

Mrs Loletta Rolle has been in Britain for 40 years and says she has totally assimilated but ... there is one little thing she simply cannot give up forever and that is her Cou-cou and Flying Fish, a dish which evokes Barbados for her. Her British-born kids do not care for it but the dish is popular with many other Barbadians and indeed is also reminiscent of similar West African dishes. Italians similarly cherish their equivalent of cou-cou – polenta!

1 First make the Cou-cou. Put half the water and half the salt into a large pan and bring to the boil. Rinse the trimmed okras under running water, trim off their tops, then slice them crossways into 0.5cm (¼in) rings. Cook, covered, for about 3 minutes or until tender.

2 Meanwhile add the remaining water and salt to the sifted cornmeal and stir well to make a smooth mixture.

3 Remove the okra from the heat and stir in the cornmeal mixture until well blended. Return the pan to a medium flame and cook, stirring all the time. When the mixture stiffens and is thick, smooth and leaves the sides of the pan as you stir, the Cou-cou is cooked. Transfer to a warmed serving dish, dot with butter, cover and keep warm.

4 Now prepare the flying fish. Bone them out and remove the gills, unless your fishmonger has done this for you. Rinse under running water, then soak in the lime juice and salted water for about 20 minutes. Drain well and pat dry.

5 To season and coat the fish, put the flour mixed with the dried herbs on a large plate and set aside. Mix half the onion, half the parsley, thyme, salt and pepper with the reserved tablespoon of lime juice and rub all over the skin and in the gut cavity of each fish. Roll each fish by taking the tail end to the head and slotting the tail fin through the gill cavity, making a ring or buckle. Dip and turn in the seasoned flour to coat and shake off any excess flour.

6 Heat the vegetable oil in a large heavy-based frying pan on a moderate flame. Fry the fish, turning them from time to time until they are evenly golden brown – about 15–20 minutes. Remove from the heat and lift out the fish, drain on crumpled kitchen paper, then put them in a warmed dish, cover with aluminium foil and keep warm.

7 Wipe out the cooled frying pan with kitchen paper, return it to the moderate flame and add the vegetable oil and butter. Add the remaining onions, herbs, chopped

tomatoes and their juices, seasoning well with salt and freshly ground black pepper. Stir-fry until the onions are soft and transparent, then add enough water to make the sauce. Simmer gently for about 20 minutes, stirring from time to time, reducing the volume to a rich creamy-textured sauce.

8   To make individual servings of the Cou-cou, put 25g (1oz) butter into a warmed deep basin, and add 3 tablespoons of the Cou-cou. Smooth into a ball and shake the mixture in the dish from side to side and backwards and forwards as it absorbs the butter. Then turn the dish upside down onto a plate and the moulded Cou-cou will slip out. Repeat this procedure for each individual serving.

9   Arrange the flying fish and Cou-cou on a warmed serving dish. Garnish with the lime or lemon wedges. Serve the sauce in a separate dish.

Variation: cold Cou-cou can be cut into slices and fried in butter or oil, until golden and crispy.

Stamp and Go

Makes about 46 fish cakes

Begin preparation a day ahead for soaking fish

700g (1¹/2lb) salt cod
2 large onions, peeled and finely chopped
1 teaspoon ground cloves
generous handful or two chopped parsley, to taste
4 teaspoons fresh thyme, to taste
2 teaspoons freshly ground black pepper, to taste
1 Scotch bonnet pepper, deseeded and very finely chopped
450g (1lb) self-raising flour
300ml (¹/2 pint) water, approximately
vegetable oil for frying

A delicious and easy Jamaican favourite which you can literally eat 'on the go'.

1   First put the salt cod into a very large basin and cover with plenty of cold water to soak for at least 12 hours or overnight. Change the water two or three times.

2   Drain the cod, put it into a saucepan with cold water to cover by 2.5–5cm (1–2in), bring to the boil, turn down the heat and simmer until tender – about 10–20 minutes. Drain in a colander, remove any skin and bones, and flake the fish into a large bowl.

3   Add the onions, cloves, parsley, thyme, pepper and Scotch bonnet pepper and use a pestle to grind the ingredients into a smooth mixture. Or use a food processor.

4   Stir the flour into the mixture to blend thoroughly. Begin to add the water gradually, stirring all the time to bind the mixture until it forms a thick and sticky batter, of just dropping consistency.

5   In a pan suitable for deep-frying, heat the vegetable oil to just under smoking point. Drop tablespoons of the mixture into the hot oil in batches of 5–10 at a time, turning them once, until they are golden brown. Do not overcrowd the pan. Remove the fish cakes and drain on kitchen paper. Serve hot or cold.

Ackee and Salt Fish Quiche

Serves 6-8

Begin preparation a day ahead for soaking fish

for the filling

3 tablespoons vegetable oil
1 medium onion, peeled and finely
   chopped
3 cloves garlic, peeled and finely
   chopped
1 chilli pepper, deseeded and finely
   chopped
1 small green capsicum pepper,
   deseeded and finely diced
350g (12oz) salt cod
1 540g (19fl oz) tin ackee
350g (12oz) mature Cheddar cheese,
   grated
300ml (½ pint) double cream
7 eggs

for the pastry

450g (1lb) pack frozen shortcrust
   pastry, thawed
   or to make pastry:
350g (12oz) plain flour
pinch salt
175g (6oz) chilled butter, diced
iced water to mix
a scrap of butter to grease the flan
   dish

In Britain, 540g tins of blanched ackee (fruit or arils as they're called) in brine are easier to get from Caribbean grocers. The tinned stuff is also safer for people who are unfamiliar with ackee because the ackee fruit can be poisonous if not picked at the correct time and treated right.

This is a Pauline Findlayson original, which she and her friend Paulette Dixon make it to mouthwatering perfection! I've made it, tasted it and I know. It is an Anglo-French twist on a Jamaican favourite. Your guests would love you for it.

1 First put the salt cod into a large basin and soak in cold water overnight. Change the water two or three times during the soaking time. Now drain the salt cod, put it into a saucepan with cold water to cover by 2.5–5cm (1–2in), bring to the boil, turn down the heat to a low flame and simmer until tender – about 10–20 minutes. Drain thoroughly in a colander, remove any skin and bones, flake the fish onto a plate and set aside. Drain the ackee, put on plate, and set aside.

2 Pre-heat the oven to 200°C/400°F/gas mark 6. Lightly butter a 30cm (12in) loose-bottomed flan dish. Use the thawed prepared shortcrust pastry, or make your own pastry in the usual way and chill it for ½ hour before using. Roll out and line the flan dish, trimming the pastry by rolling over the edge of the dish with a rolling pin. Prick the base with a fork and bake blind in the oven for about 15 minutes. Set aside to cool.

3 In a heavy-based saucepan or 'dutchy' heat up the oil and sauté the onions and garlic until transparent and soft. Add the chilli pepper and the green pepper. Continue cooking for another three minutes before adding the shredded salt fish. Cook for another minute.

4 Add the ackee. Use a fork to stir from here on so that the ackee is not crushed. Sauté for a further minute before you remove from the heat and set aside. Scatter half the grated cheese evenly over the base of the flan, then add the salt cod and ackee mixture and finish by scattering over the remaining cheese. Whisk together the cream and eggs to a light custard and carefully pour this over the top of the quiche. Bake in the oven for approximately 40 minutes, until golden brown and firm.

Salt Fish and Ackee

Begin preparation a day ahead for
soaking the salt fish

450g (1lb) salt fish
540g (19fl oz) tin ackee, drained
1–3 small green bananas or 1–2
    large plantain, peeled and sliced
1 yam, peeled and cubed
vegetable oil for frying
1 large onion, peeled and chopped
6 medium ripe tomatoes, peeled
    and chopped
generous pinch of thyme
freshly ground black pepper, to taste

to finish
quartered tomatoes, chopped parsley

Ackee is a Jamaican vegetable delicacy. It is bland by itself but beautifully complements seasoned salt cod when cooked together. There are many versions of ackee and salt fish, one of many exotic national dishes to be found in Jamaica. But this one from Mrs Clarke which incorporates root vegetables is one of the more interesting. P.S. You may also care to try ackee and pink salmon.

1 Put the salt fish into a very large basin and cover with plenty of cold water to soak for at least 12 hours or overnight. Change the water two or three times.

2 Now drain the salt fish, put it into a saucepan with cold water to cover by 2.5–5cm (1–2in), bring to the boil, turn down the heat to a low flame and simmer until tender – about 10–20 minutes. Drain thoroughly in a colander, remove any skin and bones, flake the fish onto a plate and set aside. Drain the ackee, put on to a plate, and set aside.

3 Put the prepared green bananas or plantain into salted water in a pan on a moderate to high flame, bring to the boil and cook until tender – approximately 10–15 minutes for the bananas or 15–20 minutes for the plantain. A quarter to halfway through the cooking time, add the yam to the pan so that it also cooks until tender. (Yam cooks much like potato.) Drain through a colander and leave to one side.

4 To cook the salt fish and ackee, put a large heavy-based frying pan onto a moderate flame and when hot add the oil. Tip in the onions and fry them until soft and golden. Add the tomatoes and thyme and stir-fry for a few more minutes to make a thickish sauce. Add the green bananas or plantains and yam to heat through, then push these ingredients to one side of the pan. Put the flaked salt fish into a separate part of the pan and spoon over some of the sauce to heat through. To one side of the salt fish spoon in the ackee, taking care not to crush or squash them, and spoon over a little of the sauce to heat through. Taste and adjust the seasoning with pepper (the salt fish will probably provide enough salt).

5 Spoon the finished salt fish and ackee on to a warmed serving dish and garnish with the quarters of tomato and chopped parsley. Alternatively simply garnish the pan and take it to the table. Serve with a spicy cornbread and a crisp green salad.

Jerk Chicken

Serves 4

Begin preparation at least 4 hours ahead or overnight for the marinating

*4 chicken breasts, on the bone
juice of 1/2 lemon or lime*

for the marinade
*1 onion, peeled and very finely chopped
3 spring onions, cleaned, trimmed and finely chopped
3 tablespoons soya sauce
1 teaspoon ground allspice
1 tablespoon fresh thyme leaves, chopped
1/2 tablespoon paprika
1 scotch bonnet pepper, deseeded and finely chopped
75ml (3fl oz) olive oil
2 tablespoons white wine vinegar
1 tablespoon brown sugar
2 teaspoons freshly ground black pepper*

to finish
*squeeze or two of lime juice
crisp salad leaves, lengths of spring onion, chopped parsley*

Another Jamaican winner which I'm pleased to say, is fast catching on in Britain. Jerk Chicken is a highly seasoned, spicy Jamaican 'finger-licking', barbecued/baked chicken. You can tone down or tone up the level of spiciness to suit yourself but, if up until now you have never tried this dish, shame on you. Quick, 'hoof' it down to your local grocers, buy the ingredients and get cooking before you become the odd one out! You don't have to use only chicken, you can 'jerk' anything using the same marinade. Seafood, fish, pork, vegetables ... go for it.

1 Wash the chicken pieces with the lemon or lime juice and pat dry with kitchen paper. Leave the skin on, slash the breasts in several places and put into a shallow non-metallic bowl.

2 Put all the ingredients for the marinade into the bowl of a blender or liquidiser and whizz until smooth. Smother the chicken pieces in this marinade, rubbing well into the slashes. Cover the bowl with cling film and leave in a cool place or the refrigerator for at least 4 hours, or preferably overnight, turning the pieces occasionally.

3 When you are ready to cook, preheat the oven to 180°C/350°F/gas mark 4.

4 Lift the smothered chicken pieces into a lightly oiled roasting tin and spoon over a little more of the marinade – approximately one-third of the mixture. Reserve the remaining marinade.

5 Roast the chicken in the oven for approximately 40–45 minutes, turning occasionally until thoroughly cooked and a deep golden brown – the juices should run clear when tested with a skewer.

6 Meanwhile heat the remaining marinade in a small pan on a low heat, adding a judicious squeeze or two of lime juice.

7 Arrange the Jerk Chicken on a warmed serving platter and coat with the reserved heated marinade. Surround with an attractive arrangement of salad leaves and spring onions and sprinkle the whole dish with chopped parsley. Serve with Jamaican Rice & Peas (see page 20).

Curried Goat (kid, lamb or mutton)

Serves 10

1.8kg (4lb) goat, kid, or shoulder of
  lamb or mutton, trimmed and cut
  into 3.5cm (1½in) pieces
1 tablespoon vegetable oil

for the marinade

3 tablespoons hot curry powder
2 teaspoons each of dried mixed
  herbs, ground ginger, coriander,
  ground cumin seed, fenugreek
  powder, paprika, white pepper
  and black pepper
2 tablespoons fresh coriander,
  chopped (leaves and stems)
1 tablespoon lime or lemon juice
1 teaspoon allspice
1 tablespoon soya sauce (optional)

for the vegetables

3 cloves garlic, peeled and chopped
2 large onions, peeled and chopped
4 tablespoons celery leaves, chopped
1 scotch bonnet pepper, seeded and
  finely chopped
4 potatoes, peeled and diced small
1-2 sprigs skellion, or spring onion,
  crushed and chopped

For the 'chickens' amongst you if you are too squeamish to try goat then substitute lamb or mutton/hogget but I have to tell you, whilst your dish would still taste good, it would not surfeit your culinary senses quite like a good Jamaican goat curry. Most butchers would get you goat meat if you asked, and, it is leaner, tastier and much cheaper too, I kid you not!

1 Begin preparation a day ahead or allow 12 hours for the marinade. Wash the prepared meat and pat dry with kitchen paper. Put it with the oil and all the marinade spices and herbs into a very large bowl, mix well with your hands to combine, cover the dish and leave in a cool place or in the refrigerator to marinate. Give the mixture a good stir from time to time.

2 Heat a large heavy-based pan on a moderate to hot flame. Tip in all the marinated ingredients and give a good stir as they take on some colour. Then add the garlic, onion, celery leaves and pepper and stir to incorporate into the curried meat and stir-fry for a few minutes. Add water to cover, then slide in the potatoes and skellion.

3 Turn the heat to low, cover the pan, continue to simmer gently for approximately one hour fifty minutes, stiring occasionally and adding a little more water if necessary until the meat is tender and the sauce has thickened. Serve with Basmati rice, or Jamaican Rice and peas.

Jamaican Rice and Peas

Serves 4–6

225g (8oz) red kidney beans, soaked
  overnight, or 1 450g (1lb) tin
  cooked kidney beans
1 clove garlic, peeled and crushed
600–900ml (1–1½ pints) water
1 level teaspoon salt
1 teaspoon vegetable oil
110g (4oz) block coconut cream
½ teaspoon ground black pepper
2 spring onions, trimmed and
  chopped
1 sprig fresh thyme
1 whole scotch bonnet pepper
450g (1lb) white rice

1 If using pre-soaked dried beans, drain and put into a saucepan with the garlic. Add enough water to cover the beans by about 5cm (2in). Bring to the boil, lower the flame, cover and simmer for about one hour or until tender. Then add the salt. With tinned beans, drain and put into a saucepan with the garlic. Add approximately 600ml (1 pint) water and the salt and bring to a gentle simmer on a moderate flame.

2 Add oil, coconut cream, black pepper, spring onions, thyme and the whole scotch bonnet pepper. Stir in the rice and bring back to a gentle simmer, adding a little more hot water if necessary. Turn the flame low, cover and gently simmer for approximately 20 minutes, until the rice is tender and all the liquid has been absorbed

3 Remove the scotch bonnet pepper, fluff up the rice with a fork and transfer it and the peas to a warmed serving dish.

Caribbean Beef Steaks with a Spicy Sauce

Serves 4

Begin preparation at least 12 hours ahead or overnight for the marinating

4 steaks of sirloin, best rump or fillet of beef

for the marinade

generous pinches of any or all of the following: Steak seasoning, Caribbean Seasoning, Tropical Everyday Seasoning, Herb and Spice Seasoning, Pimento Seasoning, Barbecue Seasoning, Season-all powder, available from specialist food stores and supermarkets (or: 2 teaspoons paprika, 1 teaspoon onion powder, 1 teaspoon dried mixed herbs, 1/2 teaspoon celery salt and 1/2 teaspoon garlic salt)

1 teaspoon freshly ground black pepper
1 tablespoon dark soy sauce
1 sprig fresh thyme, crumbled
1–4 cloves garlic, peeled and crushed to a purée
6 tomatoes, peeled and finely chopped in their juices or 450g (1lb) tinned tomatoes
2 medium onions, peeled and finely chopped
1 sprig skellion, crushed and chopped (if unavailable, try spring onion)
3–4 tablespoons vegetable oil, approximately

for the sauce

225g (8oz) mushrooms, sliced
450ml (3/4 pint) approximately, good beef stock
or 450ml (3/4 pint) water and a strong chicken or vegetable stock cube

This is steak with a Jamaican facelift! A little point of interest: not many black folk like to eat rare meat. In today's busy family kitchen, it is often more convenient to use prepared proprietary brands of Caribbean or Tropical seasonings, but the adventurous cook who is trying these spicy dishes for the first time might like to be creative and have fun with using various fresh seasoning that are typical of the West Indies, such as fresh thyme, celery leaves, scotch bonnet pepper, garlic and lime juice.

1 Wash the steaks and pat dry with kitchen paper. Mix together all the marinade ingredients in a roomy bowl. (It is not necessary to add salt, because this is contained in the prepared seasonings and soya sauce.) Smother the steaks in the marinade, cover with clingfilm and leave in a cool place or the refrigerator for 12 hours or overnight.

2 When you are ready to cook, heat the oil in a large heavy-based deep frying pan on a moderate to highish flame. Remove the steaks from the bowl, scraping off any marinade that is clinging to the meat. Pat dry with kitchen paper and reserve the marinade. Fry the steaks in the hot oil for a few minutes on each side until they are browned and sealed. Adjust the timing of the frying to your preference for rare, medium or well done and, whichever your preference, err on the side of under-cooking them, because they will continue to cook in their own heat whilst keeping warm as the sauce is being cooked. Use a perforated spatula to transfer the steaks to a warmed plate, cover with a 'tent' of aluminium foil and keep warm.

3 Now make the sauce. Add the mushrooms to the oil and juices in the pan and let them soften and cook gently for a minute or two. Now add the reserved marinade, the stock, or water and stock cube, and stir to amalgamate. Simmer on a low flame, reducing the volume to a rich, spicy, creamy-textured sauce, to your preferred consistency and taste. Taste and adjust the seasoning.

4 Arrange the steaks on a warmed serving platter and pour the sauce over them.

5 Serve with traditional West Indian vegetables, such as Sweet Potato (see page 23), coleslaw salad or Jamaican Rice and Peas (see page 20).

Boiled Sweet Potato

Serves 4

450g (1lb) sweet potatoes, unpeeled
300ml (¹/₂ pint) water,
  approximately
pinch salt

for the variation
50–75g (2–3oz) unsalted butter
pinch salt and freshly ground
  black pepper

Sweet potato is a staple in Caribbean cuisine. It is a versatile root vegetable which lends itself readily to sweet and savoury dishes and yet tastes good enough to eat on its own. Available in regular supermarkets, it is easy to cook but gets confused with yams, which is a shame because they are totally different.

1 Scrub the sweet potatoes under running water, but do not peel them. Put them into a large saucepan, cover with cold water, bring to the boil on a moderate flame, add the salt, cover and cook for approximately 20 minutes until tender when pierced with the point of a sharp vegetable knife or skewer. Drain through a colander.

2 When the potatoes are cool enough to handle, peel off their skins, cut into nice thick slices and arrange on a warmed dish to serve.

Fried Plantain

Serves 3-4 as an accompaniment

4 large plantains, just ripe (skins can
  be anything from green to quite
  black but should be neither 'dry
  hard' nor 'pulpy')
pinch of salt to taste
vegetable oil for frying

to finish
peanuts (optional)

Now here's an under-utilised gem of a vegetable! Plantains are a regular on the dinner tables of most black households but alas, not very well known among the general population, which is just as well or there might not be enough to go round! Although plantains are of the banana family, they cannot be eaten raw, yet they can be used in cooking whether they are green or ripe and yellow. Sometimes unripe green plantains are referred to as green bananas.

1 First peel the plantains. Cut off both ends of the plantain. Now cut through the skins lengthways, along the ridges, then peel back the segments, removing any woody fibres with a sharp vegetable knife. (Sometimes plantains release a sticky resin when peeling so you can protect your hands from staining by lightly oiling them before preparation). Slice the plantains on the diagonal into 0.5cm (¼in) slices and sprinkle with salt.

2 Heat the oil in a heavy-based frying pan over a moderate flame and fry the plantains for about 3–4 minutes on each side, turning once or twice until they are golden brown on the outside and tender and cooked on the inside. Drain on crumpled kitchen paper and serve hot with a garnish of peanuts, or as a vegetable accompaniment to dishes such as Ackee and Salt Fish (see page 18).

Spicy Vegetable Patties

Makes 10–12 patties

for the pastry
225g (8oz) plain flour
225g (8oz) self-raising flour
450g (1lb) wholewheat flour
1 teaspoon turmeric powder (for colour)
½ teaspoon salt
450g (1lb) chilled vegetable fat such as Trex or Flora, diced
chilled water to mix

for the filling
240ml (⅓ pint) corn oil
1 large onion, peeled and finely chopped
4 large cloves garlic, peeled, crushed and finely chopped
2 large carrots, peeled and very finely diced
1 large green pepper, cored, deseeded and finely diced
2 scotch bonnet peppers, deseeded and finely chopped
350g (12oz) mushrooms, wiped and very finely chopped
450g (1lb) cooked butter beans
500ml (1.6fl oz) of the butter bean cooking water
2 large sweet potatoes, peeled and finely diced
225g (8oz) uncooked sweetcorn kernels
110g (4oz) brown breadcrumbs
salt and freshly ground black pepper to taste

'Ital' means the food should be as close as possible to its natural state without additives or preservatives – and that's exactly how the kids at the Kuumba Rastafarian Centre in Bristol taught me how to make these patties which you can stuff with any spicy filling of your choosing. As vegans, the children chose the corn, mushroom, beans, potatoes, herbs and spices filling below. Make yours as spicy or as subtle as you wish.

1 First make the pastry. Sift the plain flour, self-raising flour and turmeric into a large mixing bowl, add the wholewheat flour and salt and mix together. Rub in the chilled diced vegetable fat with cool fingers, until the mixture resembles coarse breadcrumbs. Use a knife to mix in enough chilled water to gather the mixture into a soft, pliable dough. Shape it quickly into a ball, cover the bowl with a damp tea towel, or put the pastry ball into a polythene bag, and leave it in a cool place or refrigerate for ½ hour.

2 Now make the filling. Heat the corn oil in a large heavy-based pan on a moderate flame. Sweat the onion and garlic for about 5 minutes, or until they are soft and transparent. Add the carrots, pepper, scotch bonnet peppers and mushrooms and continue frying gently for a further 10–15 minutes or until all the vegetables are half cooked and becoming tender. Add the butter beans and their cooking water, then the sweet potatoes and sweetcorn. Season with salt and pepper, cover the pan, turn the flame to low, and simmer for about 20 minutes or until the sweet potatoes and sweetcorn kernels are tender. Remove from the heat, stir in the breadcrumbs and set aside to cool.

3 To make the patties, divide the chilled pastry into two or three manageable portions for rolling out on a lightly floured working surface. Roll out the first portion to a thickness of 0.5cm (¼in). Use a saucer to cut out the rounds for the patties. Put two or three teaspoons of the cooled vegetable filling on to the centre of each round and moisten the edge of each round with a little chilled water. Carefully fold over one half of each pastry round to form a crescent shaped patty. Crimp the edge with the prongs of a fork, making a decorative seal. Continue this process until all the pastry and filling are used.

4 Pre-heat the oven to 190°C/375°F/gas mark 5. Put the patties on lightly floured baking sheets, and bake in the oven for 25–35 minutes or until golden brown. Serve hot or cold. Various chutneys, or cheturney (see page 125), fresh tomato sauce and a green salad would be ideal accompaniments.

Tropical Fruit Salad de Luxe

Serves 6

for the fruit
1 small ripe pawpaw or papaya,
 peeled and cubed
4 large ripe mangoes, peeled and
 cubed
4 ripe kiwi fruit peeled and quartered
16 ripe lychees, peeled and stoned
 (if unavailable, use tinned)
1 small ripe pineapple, peeled, cored
 and cubed, reserving half for the
 marinade
1–3 tablespoons caster sugar to taste
 (optional)

for the marinade/sauce
½ small ripe pineapple, peeled,
 cored and cubed (see above)
8 ripe passionfruit, juices and seeds
 scooped out
250ml (6 fl oz) triple sec or
 Cointreau (optional)
125ml (¼ pint) chilled water,
 approximately

This is a simple but effective twist on the traditional fruit salad. Combine as many fresh exotic tropical fruits as possible.

1 Put all the prepared fruits into a large glass or china serving bowl and sprinkle over the sugar to taste (if using).

2 For the marinade, put the cubed pineapple into the bowl of a liquidiser or blender and pulse to a purée, add the juices and seeds of the passion fruit and give one or two more pulses. Combine this purée with the alcohol (if using) and the chilled water and pour over the cubed fruits. Stir, taking care not to crush.

3 Cover the bowl with clingfilm and chill for several hours in the refrigerator. Serve in chilled dishes, with fresh cream, yoghurt, or just as it is.

Guinness Punch

Serves 4

125ml (4fl oz) dark rum
110g (4oz) brown sugar
1 400g (14oz) tin evaporated milk
1 400g (14oz) tin condensed milk
1 teaspoon angostura bitters
1 teaspoon vanilla essence

to finish
2 440ml (15fl oz) cans Guinness or
 similar stout
crushed ice
½ teaspoon freshly grated nutmeg

This can be very sweet with both the condensed milk and the brown sugar so if you are not very sweet-toothed, I suggest you omit the sugar. It is a misleading drink, because it tastes so good (like a milk shake), it is easy to forget it is alcoholic. Do not drive after you drink Guinness Punch!

1 Put the first six ingredients into a punch bowl and stir well to mix. Slowly stir in the Guinness or stout.

2 Put a generous amount of crushed ice into chilled glasses, pour in the Guinness Punch, sprinkle with nutmeg and serve.

Spicy Mincemeat & Apple Tart

Serves 6

for the pastry
225g (8oz) self-raising flour
50g (2oz) plain flour
pinch salt
150g (5oz) margarine, chilled
and diced
2 teaspoons sugar
1 egg yolk
chilled water to bind
1–2 teaspoons caster sugar for
sprinkling on the pastry

for the filling
5 cooking apples, peeled, cored and
finely chopped
1 teaspoon ground mixed spice
pinch of cinnamon powder
1 large jar mincemeat

a scrap or two of margarine to
grease the flan dish

Loletta Rolle served me this on our first meeting and I fell in love with it. When I was growing up in Ghana, mother and my aunties used to buy me a version of this in packets but ours had no apples, just the minced fruit mix, which, pressed between the pastry slices, looked just like squashed flies and that is exactly what we called them, 'Squashed Flies'. The name does them no justice: they're delicious.

1 First make the pastry. Sift the two flours and salt into a mixing bowl. Rub in the margarine with cool fingers and thumbs, until the mixture resembles fine breadcrumbs. Stir in the sugar and egg yolk, then use a knife to mix in enough chilled water to bind, and gather the mixture into a soft, pliable dough. Do not overhandle the pastry; shape it quickly into a ball, cover the bowl with a damp tea towel or put the pastry ball into a polythene bag and leave it in a cool place to rest for ½ hour. Grease a flan or tart dish and set aside.

2 Preheat oven to 190°C/375°F/gas mark 5.

3 To make the tart, take half of the pastry and roll it out on a lightly floured working surface, turning the pastry as you work to form a circle the size of the tart or flan dish. Line the dish with the pastry, trim the edges, and prick the base with a fork. Spread the mincemeat over the base, cover with the diced apple, and sprinkle with the spice and cinnamon. Brush the edge of the pastry base with a little chilled water. Roll out the remaining pastry for the lid, then lift it into position to cover the tart. Seal the edge of the tart by pressing the two edges together, crimp and seal with the prongs of a fork, and trim excess pastry from the edge of the tart. Prick the pastry lid in the centre, for the steam to escape when baking.

4 Bake in the oven for 40–45 minutes, until lightly browned. Remove from the oven, sprinkle with the sugar and, when cool, cut into slices for serving.

Chapter 2: Greek

It is hard to get a handle on the London Greeks. Are they European, as their language would suggest, or Middle-Eastern, like their food? Are they aristocratic shipping millionaires or ordinary working people struggling in the city to make a living from catering and the rag trade? Do they hate their bitter rivals the Turks, as foreign correspondents tell us, or get along with them just fine, as they appear to on the streets of London where they live as neighbours, eating the same food and shopping in the same shops? And lastly, why, when you go to Greece on holiday, is the food completely different from the Greek food you've eaten here in Britain? I have plenty of questions, and I don't know if I can answer them all. But I can surely try... so here goes!

The main source of these paradoxes is simple: the great majority of the Greeks in Britain are not from mainland Greece but from the lovely island of Cyprus, tucked neatly away in a corner of the Mediterranean between Turkey and Lebanon. They share the island, rather uneasily it must be said, with Turkish Cypriots. The geographical position of the place is the key to their style of cooking. They have wine in abundance, but in most other respects their cuisine is Levantine. Look at a book on Middle Eastern food and you'll find variations on all the Greek Cypriot themes. Greece itself feels a long way North and West, and that's why holidaymakers look in vain for their humous, sheftalia and moussaka.

Another paradox: 'Greek' food is often considered simple and unsophisticated. What's a kebab? A few pieces of grilled meat in an envelope of bread – you can't get much simpler than that, can you? And yet, when you take a good look in a Greek grocer's in

Michael's Fruiterer's in the Seven Sisters Road, London, a veritable haven of goodies.

Mr Philippos and his acres of filo pastry.

Haringey, you see cheeses like halomi, kefalotiri, feta and ricotta (which they call 'anari'), big bunches of fresh herbs – parsley, coriander and basil – and a cornucopia of vegetables. Alongside all the in-season English vegetables, there are capsicum peppers (including smaller, wrinkly ones, and long thin ones of all shades of green, orange and red, and infinitely varying piquancy), chillies, artichoke, aubergine, fabulous big misshapen quinces, squashes of various strange shapes and colours, and real Cypriot specialities like kolokassi, a big, rough-skinned, off-white tuber reminiscent of Caribbean dasheen and our very own West African cocoyam. Kolokassi is delicious braised with pork (see page 36).

Pork, chicken and especially lamb are the mainstay of the great Greek barbecue, a regular feature of extended-family life – when we get anything vaguely resembling Cypriot weather, that is. The smoking coals and grill laden with succulent meat provide a focal point and some drama and atmosphere for the party. The smell is all-important: after all, that's what attracted the gods of ancient Greece down from Mount Olympus to witness sacrifices being roasted in their honour. While the patriarch is busying himself with the fire, the matriarch is covering the big trestle table with crusty round loaves of freshly baked bread, green salad, Greek salad, tzadziki, olives and dolmades – exquisite stuffing wrapped in leaves from the very same vine which hangs over the table providing welcome shade for the waiting lunch. In Greek hands the barbecue is an art-form, and I fancy that they must be partly responsible for its massive popularity in Australia and the USA.

Apart from food, the force which holds the Greek community together is the Orthodox Church. Even if young people are not as devout as their parents or grandparents through the year, everyone, but everyone, celebrates Easter. On Good Friday, the coffin of Christ – the epitaphion – is carried around the streets followed by a chanting procession. Late Saturday evening often sees a colourful mass in the church, with a candle lit by every member of the congregation as a blessing for the year ahead, the air heavy with incense and the hypnotic incantation of prayers. Around midnight the people go home or out to eat. This is the end of a strictly-observed Lent, and time to catch up on some meat and dairy products. They take with them from the church hard-boiled eggs, painted red for the blood of Christ. Lunch on Easter day is, need I say it, barbecue time.

The Greeks who live in Britain are proud of their traditional food. There are companies who make humous, taramasalata and filo pastry: there are wonderful Greek grocers, and many good Greek restaurants. Some say that you can eat better, and more authentically, in London than in Cyprus itself. I don't know about that, but I do know that you can have a very good Greek party if you try some of these excellent recipes, courtesy of the many Greek Cypriot friends I made during the filming of my television series.

Avgolemono

Serves 6–8

1 whole chicken, jointed
2.3 litres (4 pints) water or vegetable
 or chicken stock
225g (8oz) long grain rice
salt and freshly ground black pepper

for the Avgolemono
4 large eggs, preferably free-range,
 room temperature
250ml (8fl oz) water
juice of 3 large lemons

Avgolemono is a traditional, favourite Greek soup usually eaten after the midnight service on Greek Easter Saturday. It is a simple soup – just lemon, chicken stock, rice, eggs and seasoning – but it tastes magnificent. The trick here is to ensure the beaten eggs are sufficiently warmed before you add them to the hot stock or they curdle! I spent last Easter with Goula (pronounced goolah), her husband Michael, their children and Goula's parents, Anna and Ronnie, aunty Christaleni, grandma Kyriacou, sisters Loulla and Alex and I tasted my first avgolemono. I had two helpings! Anna is a great cook so after the church service, I invited myself round to learn how to cook this delicious soup and flaones, another example of traditional Easter fare. Avgolemono is so traditional it is considered 'de rigueur' at Easter; an excellent way to break the fast of Lent.

1 Trim and rinse the chicken pieces under running water. Put them with the water or stock into a large heavy-based pan on a moderate flame. If using water, add salt and pepper. If stock, allow for salt and seasonings already included in the stock, taste and check the seasoning at the end of the cooking time. Bring to simmering point, skim any froth from the surface, partially cover the pan and poach the chicken for about 30–35 minutes, skimming occasionally until the broth is clear.

2 Now add the rice and continue gently simmering for a further 10 minutes until the rice and chicken are cooked. Lift the chicken pieces from the pan, transfer to a warmed dish, cover and keep warm. Taste and adjust the seasoning and keep the rice and stock on a low flame, just under simmering point.

3 To make the Avgolemono, crack the eggs (which must be room temperature) into a large mixing bowl and whisk thoroughly. Add the water and whisk for a further 2–3 minutes, then add the lemon juice and whisk until you have a light frothy mixture.

4 It is very important not to add boiling hot broth to the mixture. Take a ladleful of the broth from pan and very slowly pour it into the eggs, whisking all the time to amalgamate, then add another ladleful in the same way. Now pour the egg mixture into the pan, off the heat. Reheat very gently and stir until the sauce thickens – about 3–4 minutes. Taste and add a squeeze of more lemon juice if necessary.

5 Serve the chicken pieces with the sauce, a fresh green salad and Greek bread.

Dashi

Serves 2–4

6 tablespoons tahini (sesame paste)
1 tablespoon water
juice of 1–2 lemons
1–2 cloves garlic, crushed, peeled
    and chopped
2 tablespoons Greek olive oil
salt and freshly ground black pepper

to finish
1 tablespoon flat-leaf parsley

One of the easiest dips to make in a hurry. I keep a jar of tahini in my cupboard at the ready in case of emergency. This, and the following four recipes, are appetisers, so vary the proportions according to the number of people.

1 Put the tahini into a mixing bowl, add the water and beat with a whisk to lighten the consistency of the tahini paste. Now, using the whisk, gradually beat in the lemon juice and add the garlic. Continue beating while trickling in the olive oil until the mixture is smooth and creamy. Season to taste with salt and pepper. Pour into a bowl to serve as dip, garnished with flat-leaf parsley.

Fried Halumi

Serves 2–4

1 packet halumi cheese
4 tablespoons Greek olive oil

Another emergency stand-by, halumi has gained popularity recently. It is now trendy to include it as an appetiser or serve as the beginning of a light lunch.

1 Remove the halumi cheese from the packet, drain and cut into 1cm (½in) slices. Heat 3 tablespoons of the oil in a heavy-based frying pan and fry the slices of halumi for about 2 minutes on each side until golden brown. Lift the slices from the pan, arrange on a warmed plate and drizzle over the remaining tablespoon of olive oil. Serve at once.

Humous Me Tahini

Serves 2–4

Begin soaking the chickpeas a day
ahead

450g (1lb) cooked and drained
    chickpeas, cooking water reserved
6 tablespoons tahini (sesame paste)
2 cloves garlic, crushed, peeled and
    chopped
juice of 1 lemon
salt and freshly ground black pepper
3 tablespoons of Greek olive oil
handful of chopped flat-leaf parsley

I love this dip. For years, as soon the sun reared its head, I lived on my favourite summer combination – humous, tabouleh and pitta bread. It is so tasty and light and, for once, good for you. This is a recipe given to me by my Greek Cypriot friend Mary Spyrou, with whom I filmed the making of dolmades (see page 35). I put everything bar the parsley in a blender, but you can use a large pestle and mortar.

1 Put the chickpeas in a large pan, covered with water, bring to the boil and skim until the liquid is clear. Cover and cook until soft, takes about 1 hour. Strain, reserving the liquid, and cool. Put the chickpeas and some cooking liquid into a liquidiser and purée, gradually adding the tahini, garlic, lemon juice and olive oil to make a creamy paste. Put the batches of mixture into a bowl, stir to combine and beat in a little more of the cooking water, lemon juice and olive oil. Season to taste. Drizzle over some olive oil and garnish with the flat-leaf parsley.

Talatouri/Tsadziki

Serves 2-4

1 carton Greek yoghurt
1/4–1/2 cucumber, peeled and cut into
  0.5cm (1/2in) dice
2 teaspoons fresh mint leaves,
  chopped, or dried mint leaves,
  crushed
1 clove garlic, crushed, peeled and
  chopped or pounded to a purée
salt and freshly ground black pepper
  (optional)
pinch of paprika

This is probably one of the better-known dips; most people make it with just yoghurt and cucumber but I think the mint makes it more refreshing and is a good aid to the digestion.

Pour the yoghurt into a bowl and beat with a fork. If the yoghurt dip is not to be eaten soon, it is advisable to salt the cucumber and leave it to drain in a colander before mixing with the yoghurt, or the dip will become watery. Pat the cucumber dry with kitchen paper. Stir into the yoghurt, add the mint, season with salt and pepper (if using). Serve in small dishes, sprinkled with paprika and garnish with a leaf or two of fresh mint.

Taramasalata

Serves 2-4

110–150g (4–5oz) smoked cod's roe
  (or smoked roe of grey mullet –
  rarely available)
2–4 slices day old bread, crust
  removed, soaked briefly in water
  or 2–4 potatoes, cooked and
  mashed
1 clove garlic, crushed, peeled and
  roughly chopped
juice of 1–2 lemons
6-8 tablespoons Greek olive oil
a little water (optional)

to serve

1 teaspoon paprika
1 tablespoon finely chopped flat-leaf
  parsley
warm pitta bread

This is a favourite with many people but the home-made version is often creamy and salmon pink in colour whereas the shop version is bright pink. Well, my Greek Cypriot friend Mahi Theo told me the secret – beetroot juice, yes, beetroot juice is blended into the finished product to intensify the colour to make it more appealing. So now you know. Frankly, I'm relieved to hear this because I thought the commercial variety used food colouring.

1 Wrap the roe in a piece of muslin, put into a bowl, and soak in water for about 10–15 minutes to reduce the saltiness.

2 Drain the roe, remove the skin and put it into the bowl of a blender or liquidiser. Squeeze the bread dry, add this (or the potatoes) to the roe with the garlic and start the motor running. Gradually trickle in the olive oil and process until the mixture is a pale pink creamy mixture, the consistency of thick mayonnaise. Add the lemon juice to taste and whizz to amalgamate. Pour into a bowl and check the taste. More olive oil or lemon juice may be added, or the tarama can be lightened a little by beating in 1–2 tablespoons of water.

3 To finish the dish, drizzle over a little olive oil, sprinkle with paprika and chopped parsley, and serve with warm pitta bread.

Dolmades

1 packet of vine leaves in brine

for the stuffing
3 tablespoons Greek olive oil
1 medium onion, peeled and very
    finely chopped
1–2 cloves garlic, crushed, peeled
    and very finely chopped
1 small green pepper, cored,
    deseeded and very finely chopped
1 small red pepper, cored, deseeded
    and very finely chopped
450g (1lb) ripe tomatoes, peeled,
    deseeded and finely diced
2 cloves, crushed and pounded to a
    powder
2.5cm (1in) stick cinnamon, crushed
    and pounded to a powder
1 tablespoon flat-leaf parsley, finely
    chopped
110g (4oz) rice
good pinch salt and freshly ground
    black pepper
good squeeze of fresh lemon juice

for the layers of Dolmades
1–2 cloves garlic, crushed, peeled
    and cut into slivers

for cooking the Dolmades
150ml (¼ pint) water, approximately
150ml (¼ pint) Greek olive oil
juice of 1 lemon

to serve
wedges of lemon

A popular and versatile Greek dish, it can be made both as vegetarian as given below or with minced meat added as an optional extra. I had a lovely afternoon making and filming this with Mary Spyrou and Mahi Theo. It is time consuming but well worth the effort because the home-made variety tastes completely different.

1 Open the packet of vine leaves and soak in a basin of boiling water for about 20 minutes, then drain in a colander, rinse under running cold water and set aside. (If fresh young vine leaves are available, these can be blanched for 1–2 minutes, drained and set aside.) Prepare and assemble the remaining ingredients.

2 Heat the oil in a large heavy-based pan on a moderate flame. Add the onion and fry gently for 1–2 minutes, then add the garlic and continue cooking until soft and pale. Add the peppers and stir to coat them with the oil. Stir in the tomatoes and continue cooking gently for about 5 minutes.

3 Now add the spices, parsley and rice. Season, add the lemon juice and mix well. Cook for a further 2 minutes, remove from the heat and allow the mixture to cool. (The partially cooked rice will continue to cook in the stuffed vine leaves.)

4 Lightly grease a heavy-based pan with olive oil and line with a few vine leaves.

5 Place a vine leaf at a time on the working surface, stem towards you, veined side up. Put about one teaspoon of the stuffing on the centre of the leaf, fold over the leaf from the stem end. Fold in the sides and roll to make a loose parcel, allowing space for the rice as it cooks and swells. Layer the stuffed vine leaves tightly in the prepared pan, tucking in slivers of garlic here and there. Cover with spare vine leaves or some lettuce leaves.

6 Put the pan on a low flame, just cover the Dolmades with the combined cooking liquids and bring up to a gentle simmer. To keep the Dolmades in place put a small plate on top of them and cover the pan with a tight-fitting lid. Simmer for about 1 hour. Check that the cooking liquid is not drying out – if necessary add a little boiling water. Remove the pan from the heat, allow it to cool completely. Lift the Dolmades out of the pan and serve cold with wedges of lemon.

Pork braised with Kolokassi

Serves 6

900g (2lb) shoulder of pork, boned, trimmed and cut into bite-sized pieces
1–2 tablespoons seasoned flour
5 tablespoons sunflower oil
1 large onion, peeled and finely chopped
3–4 sticks celery, coarsely chopped
1 400g (14oz) tin of tomatoes, liquidised to a purée, with an equal amount of water added
2 tablespoons tomato purée
900g (2lb) kolokassi (see page 29)
juice of 1–2 lemons
good pinch or two of salt and freshly ground black pepper
300ml (½ pint) good well-flavoured stock, red wine, or just water – or enough to cover the meat and kolokassi

to serve

handful of flat-leaf parsley, finely chopped

Kolokassi is a delicious, staple, root vegetable in Greek Cypriot cooking. It is of the taro or cocoyam family. It is starchy, grows underground and is largely cultivated for its roots. Although like the others kolokassi looks brown and fibrous, it is easily distinguishable from the rest because it is much larger, with a distinct white stump at one end, and it has circular scars over its body where smaller, edible tubers have been broken off for other uses. Scientifically, it is of the *Araceae* family and the Latin name is *Colocasia antiquorum*.

Typically Cypriot food, this delicious recipe was given to me by Mahi Theo. When cooked with just stock or plain water, it needs a bit more body, but this can be rectified by using red wine instead. Also, use a shoulder of pork for extra succulence; modern, lean pork is too dry for this type of dish.

1 First prepare and trim the pork, rinse the pieces and pat dry with kitchen paper. Put them into a large polythene bag with the seasoned flour; hold the neck of the bag and give it a good shake to coat the pork lightly with the flour.

2 Heat the oil in a large heavy-based pan on a moderate to hot flame. Briskly fry the meat in small batches, turning them as they take on a golden brown colour. Do not overcrowd the pan, or the meat will steam and become soggy. Remove and drain on kitchen paper.

3 Lower the heat to a moderate flame, add the onion and celery, stir-fry until the onion is soft and transparent and the celery is nearly tender. Stir in the tomatoes, water and tomato purée and bring to boiling point. Return the meat to the pan, lower the heat and simmer gently for ½ hour.

4 If the kolokassi are very large, cut them into convenient-sized pieces for peeling with a vegetable knife. Wipe with a damp cloth or kitchen paper. (Wear rubber gloves to hold the kolokassi because it is a very sticky vegetable and difficult to grasp with bare hands! Do not rinse or wash with water as this will make it slimy and even more difficult to hold.) Use a small sharp vegetable knife to chip off small slivers of the kolokassi, adding a sprinkling of lemon juice as you work to prevent discoloration.

5 Now tip the kolokassi slivers on top of the simmering pork and add enough of the stock, wine or water just to cover. Add the lemon juice, salt and pepper, cover the pan and continue to cook gently for a further 30–40 minutes. Shake the pan from time to time but do not stir.

6 If the sauce is a little too thin at the end of the cooking time, use a perforated spoon to transfer the pork and kolokassi to a warmed serving dish and continue cooking the sauce at a brisk simmer until it thickens. Check the seasoning. Then pour the sauce over the pork and kolokassi.

7 Sprinkle with chopped parsley and serve with accompaniments (Mrs Theo's would include long radishes, koupepia, dolmades, white yam).

Spatchcocked Quails with Lemon & Greek Salad

Serves 4

Allow 2–4 hours for marinating

4 quails

for the marinade
2–3 teaspoons sea salt
freshly ground black pepper
juice of 3 lemons
50ml (2fl oz) Greek olive oil
240ml (8fl oz) red wine

for the salad
1 large cos lettuce, washed and torn
    into pieces
1 medium onion, peeled and thinly
    sliced into rings
4 spring onions, washed, trimmed
    and sliced on the diagonal
1/2 cucumber, washed and thinly
    sliced
3 large ripe tomatoes, washed and
    quartered
1/2 green pepper, cored, deseeded
    and sliced into long strips
handful of fresh mint leaves, washed
225g (8oz) feta cheese, cubed
110g (4oz) black olives

for the dressing
4 tablespoons Greek olive oil
4 tablespoons white wine vinegar
salt and freshly ground black pepper

Quails are very popular fare in Greek cuisine. Unlike chicken, skewered bar-becued quails are light and form a good partnership with Greek salad.

1 First, wash the quails and pat them dry with kitchen paper. Use kitchen scissors or game shears to cut each bird down the back without cutting the breast, open them up and spread them out on the working surface, skin side up. Press them down gently to flatten. Make a slit in the base of each thigh with a sharp knife. Double back each drumstick and insert the ends of them into the slits.

2 Combine the marinade ingredients in a large shallow non-metallic dish, smother the birds in this mixture and leave them, covered, in the dish to marinate in a cool place or in the refrigerator for 2–4 hours.

3 For the salad, put the first seven ingredients into a bowl and toss to combine. Put the dressing ingredients into a screw top jar and shake to mix. Do not dress the salad until you are ready to serve.

4 Light the barbecue or pre-heat the grill and get it good and hot. Run two metal skewers crossways through each bird to secure and hold in position when grilling. Put the quails over the hot coals or under the grill and turn them as they cook to a golden brown. When the juices run clear when pricked with a skewer, the birds are cooked.

5 Toss the salad in the dressing and scatter in the feta cheese and olives. Serve with the hot quails and warm pitta bread.

Greek-style Fish Salad with Mayonnaise

Serves 4–6 as a main course, 6–8 as an appetiser

for the fish
900g (2lb) fresh fillet of cod or hake
2 steaks of fresh salmon (or one tin of the best)

for the aromatic stock
3 medium potatoes, peeled and quartered
2 medium carrots, peeled and sliced
1 medium onion, peeled and sliced
2 sticks of celery, scrubbed and sliced
2 sprigs parsley, bruised
6 peppercorns
4 cloves
1 bay leaf
3 tablespoons white wine vinegar or lemon juice

for the dressing
6-8 tablespoons lemon juice
6-8 tablespoons Greek olive oil
good pinch salt, freshly ground black pepper

for the mayonnaise
2 egg yolks
1 whole egg
1 teaspoon mustard powder
1 tablespoon white wine vinegar
300ml (½ pint) sunflower oil
300ml (½ pint) Greek olive oil
juice of 1–2 lemons
salt and freshly ground white pepper to taste

for the garnish
ribbons of lettuce, gherkins, tomato roses, halved black or green olives, quartered hard-boiled eggs, prawns, strips of red pepper, chopped flat-leaf parsley and wedges of lemon

Mahi Theo is a sprightly, elegant Greek Cypriot lady from North London whose looks belie her years. She is generous to a fault and will not stop feeding you from the moment you walk in the door till you leave! I feel privileged to have been given this recipe to pass on. I have never seen fish prepared like this before but it tasted delicious. Treat the fish with tender loving care as Mahi does so it does not disintegrate in the poaching process.

1 First, wash the fish, pat dry with kitchen paper, remove any stray bones, remove skin if desired (though the skin may be left on while poaching, to prevent the fillet from falling apart), and set aside.

2 Put all the ingredients for the stock into a large, shallow, heavy-based pan on a moderate flame, add water just to cover and bring to the boil. Turn the flame down slightly and simmer gently for 15 minutes. If the potatoes are already tender and cooked at this stage, remove them with a perforated spoon and set aside: otherwise they can remain in the poaching liquid while the fish cooks.

3 Arrange the fish on top of the simmering vegetables, cover the pan and gently poach the fish, at just under simmering point for about 5–10 minutes, perhaps 15 minutes at the most, or until the fish is very nearly cooked. The timing will depend on the thickness of the fillets. Remove the pan from the heat and leave the fish to cool in the stock, which will complete the cooking of the fish.

4 When completely cool use a perforated spatula to lift the fish and potatoes carefully from the pan. Flake the fish and set aside. Add drained tin of salmon if using. Cube the potatoes, dress with the combined lemon juice, olive oil, salt and pepper and set aside.

5 To make the mayonnaise, put the whole egg and two yolks, the mustard powder and white wine vinegar into the bowl of a blender or liquidiser. Whizz to amalgamate, then begin to add the oil, a few drops at a time to start with, then in a steady trickle, keeping the machine running as the mayonnaise thickens and becomes pale and creamy. Check for taste, add lemon juice and seasonings to taste.

6 Now put half the mayonnaise into a bowl, gently fold in the flaked fish, put the mixture on to a large oval serving dish and spread it out evenly, leaving a border all around the dish. Pour and spread the rest of the mayonnaise all over the fish.

7 Put the ribbons of lettuce all around the border, dot with gherkins, tomato roses, olives, prawns, hard-boiled eggs, strips of red pepper and wedges of lemon. Sprinkle with the flat-leaf parsley and serve as a main course or an appetiser.

Bamies Me Domaties

450g (1lb) tender young okra, trimmed
4 tablespoons Greek olive oil
1 medium onion, peeled and finely chopped
1 clove garlic, crushed, peeled and chopped
450g (1lb) ripe tomatoes, peeled and chopped
1 bay leaf
salt and freshly ground black pepper
juice of 1 lemon

They're called okra or bamie or okro/ochro or gumbo or Syrian mallow or gombo depending on your nationality but whatever name you choose, okra is an acquired taste. Its slender, tapered green pods are filled with small, round, edible seeds and the vegetable can be quite glutinous in preparation, but there are ways around it such as keeping them dry in preparation and adding lemon or lime juice to the cooking. You either love it or hate it, there is no half-way house. Of the people who love this most distinct vegetable, and I am one of them – here's a surprise for you. Did you know that okra belongs to the hibiscus family? Well, it does, indeed its botanic name is *Hibiscus esculentus*. Here is an easy, tempting recipe from Mary Spyrou to start you off on a lifetime love affair with okra.

1 Wash the okra and pat dry with kitchen paper.

2 Heat up the olive oil in a large shallow heavy-based pan and gently fry the onion and garlic until soft and translucent. Add the okra, gently fry them for about 5 minutes, then add the tomatoes, bay leaf, salt and freshly ground black pepper and the lemon juice. Continue cooking, simmering for a further 15–20 minutes during which time the sauce will reduce to a thick, well-flavoured tomato sauce.

Flaounes

Makes about 12

for the filling

450g (1lb) Flaounes cheese, finely grated (if unavailable, use one-third grated Halumi, one-third grated Cheddar and one-third grated firm cheese, eg sheep's cheese)
2 tablespoons fine semolina
1 large egg, beaten
1 tablespoon sugar
3 teaspoons pine resin (Masticha) finely pounded
3 teaspoons cherry pips (Mechelbi) freshly ground (both available in Greek/Cypriot foodstores)
1 tablespoon fresh mint leaves, finely chopped
2 tablespoons raisins
½ teaspoon salt, to taste
1 tablespoon baking powder

for the pastry jackets

700g (1½lb) plain flour
110g (4oz) butter
½ teaspoon salt
warm water to mix
150g (5oz) sesame seeds
1 egg, beaten

Flaounes are as traditional at Greek Easter in Cyprus as Christmas pudding is at Christmas. Neither occasion would be complete without these sweets and they are each as time-consuming and distinctive in make-up as the other. Flaounes, though, are quite dry and I understand from my hosts that it is not considered rude to dunk them in a good cup of tea or coffee!

1 Put the grated cheese(s) into a mixing bowl with the semolina. mix well and set aside for about 30 minutes. giving an occasional stir so that the semolina absorbs the oils from the cheese. The resulting texture should be firm: the semolina will help to bind and give body to the filling.

2 Add the egg. stir well to combine. then add in the sugar. Masticha. Mechelbi. finely chopped mint. raisins and last of all the salt and baking powder. Mix to form a light soft dough. shape into a ball. cover the bowl and set aside for 20–30 minutes.

3 Meanwhile make the pastry. Sift the flour and salt into a large mixing bowl. rub in the butter with your fingers and thumbs until the mixture resembles fine breadcrumbs. Use a knife to mix enough warm water to bind and gather the mixture into a soft pliable dough. Do not overhandle the pastry; shape it quickly into a ball. cover the bowl with a damp tea towel or put the pastry into a polythene bag and leave to relax for ½ hour.

4 Set the oven to 180°C/350°F/gas mark 4. Lightly butter a baking sheet.

5 Take a tennis-ball sized portion of the dough. roll it out on a lightly floured working surface to a thickness of 0.3cm (⅛in) and trim to a square of about 12.5–15cm (5–6in). Sprinkle some of the sesame seeds on a clean area of the working surface. lift the pastry square on to the sesame seeds and press it down gently so that the seeds become embedded in what will become the outer side of the pastry jacket.

6 Pinch off a table tennis-ball sized portion of the filling. Put it in the middle of the pastry square. To form the Flaounes first fold over the top edge of the pastry almost to the centre of the filling. then do the same with the bottom edge and repeat with the edges to right and left. making sure that some of the filling is showing at the top of the pastry jacket. Trim the pastry. use the prongs of a fork to gently crimp and seal the seams of the pastry. and transfer to the baking sheet. Repeat the process with the remaining pastry and filling until all the ingredients are used. Brush the tops with beaten egg and bake in the oven for about 30–40 minutes until golden crisp. Serve hot or cold – with a hot strong Greek coffee.

Galatoboureko

Serves at least 12
(it's a party dish)

for the cream filling
225g (8oz) fine semolina
6 tablespoons cornflour
350g (12oz) sugar
1.5 litres (2½ pints) milk
40g (1½oz) butter
6 eggs
pinch salt
few drops vanilla essence, to taste
250g (8oz) chopped almonds
   (optional)

for the pastry
450g (1lb) pack frozen filo pastry,
   thawed
175g (6oz) melted butter or
   sunflower oil

for the syrup
300ml (½ pint) water
450g (1lb) sugar
1 tablespoon lemon juice
1 stick cinnamon broken in two
3–4 cloves
1–2 tablespoons blossom water

1 First make the cream filling. Put the semolina, cornflour and half of the sugar into a large basin and mix to a paste with a little of the milk. Bring the remaining milk to the boil on a medium flame. Pour a little of the hot milk into the paste, stirring well to amalgamate, adding more milk gradually until the mixture reaches pouring consistency. Then pour the mixture back into the milk pan and stir continuously with a balloon whisk on a low flame until the cream is smooth and free of lumps. Stir in the butter, draw off the heat and leave until lukewarm.

2 Meanwhile, using a mixer or hand whisk, whisk the eggs, pinch of salt and remaining sugar until pale, frothy and slightly thickened and then add a few drops of vanilla essence. Add the whisked eggs to the lukewarm cream (if the cream is still hot, the eggs may curdle), stirring continuously. Cover the cream, set it aside until completely cool.

3 Preheat oven to 190°C/375°F/gas mark 5. Select a baking tin with deepish sides, about 10cm (4in), measuring about 37 x 25cm (15 x 10in). Brush the tin liberally with some of the melted butter or oil. Carefully unwrap and unroll the stacks of filo pastry, measure and cut to just over the length of the baking tin but do not worry too much about the width. Lay one leaf of the filo pastry over the bottom of the tin, brush it with melted butter or oil, and repeat with the next five leaves, buttering or oiling each leaf except the last one. (Keep the stack of filo pastry covered with a damp tea towel as you work, to prevent it drying out and becoming brittle.)

4 Pour in the cooled cream mixture and smooth it over gently. Scatter over the chopped almonds. Cover with the next leaf of filo, brushing with the butter or oil, and continue the layering and buttering process with the remaining five leaves. Brush the top with butter or oil, fold over the edges and butter or oil these too. Sprinkle all over with a few drops of water to prevent the edges from curling.

5 Using a sharp knife, carefully score through the top leaves to form diamond shapes, about 5–7.5cm (2–3in). Don't cut into the almonds. Bake for 40–50 minutes until golden brown. Turn the oven up for the final 10 minutes to brown the dish if necessary.

6 Meanwhile, boil the water, sugar, lemon juice, cinnamon and cloves for at least 10 minutes. Strain into a jug to cool and add the blossom water.

7 When the Galatoboureko is cooked, carefully pour over half the syrup, let it seep in and settle for 10 minutes and then pour over the remaining syrup. Let it stand for a further 10 minutes, then cut into the diamonds and lift out individually to serve warm or cold. Keeps well, covered in a cool place for two or three days.

Chapter 3: Chinese

When the Union Jack was lowered in Hong Kong in 1997, everybody took notice; it ended the last chapter in the history of British colonialism. But it had an extra special meaning for the Chinese community in this country, most of whom came originally from Hong Kong. The story had started 250 years ago with the British addiction to tea; they traded with China, went to war with China, and took Hong Kong as their foothold in the region. Today the British may not have their colony there, but they drink just as much tea as ever, and they also eat a great deal of Chinese food. In Britain you are never (I am pleased to say) very far from a Chinese restaurant. Recently I visited a Chinese food factory in Manchester which produces two tons of noodles per hour, and an enormous Chinese supermarket – one of several which have outgrown the city centre and gone out-of-town.

Manchester seems to have taken over from Liverpool as the Chinese capital of the North; and of course London has a major Chinatown in Soho. During the working week Chinese people may be doing their business all over the place, but on Sundays they love to get together in these centres to speak Chinese, feast on Chinese food, and just be Chinese.

Community and family are at the core of Chinese life. This helps to explain one of the many conundrums of their style of cuisine: why so many different little dishes? Rather than each person with a private plate of their own, the Chinese family spreads all those dishes around the table and shares. That also explains why they don't go for a series of courses; everything is put out at once, and you can combine the bits as you please. The almost proverbial politeness of the Chinese means that, so far from a free-for-all, this is a chance to show consideration by passing things round and offering the best morsels to your loved ones.

And what morsels! Such variety and such complexity! Of course China is a big country, and the regions are very different. Canton is the standard that we all know and love; Szechwàn is famous for hot, spicy foods; Peking is thought of as delicate and sophisticated. Rice prevails in the South; grain for noodles, dumplings and pancakes in the North. Then there's four thousand years of culinary tradition; that's long enough to work out a few variations, isn't it? In 1100BC at the Imperial Court they had a medical officer who was a dietician. And these are people who love

Wing and the answer to his prayers.

tradition, who worship their ancestors. So recipes don't just come and go; when a new one is invented, it stays invented!

Of course the Chinese have almost as many proverbs as recipes, and one of them says, 'Live close to the sea and you come to know about fish, live close to the mountains and you come to know about birds, live close to the kitchen and you come to know about good food.' In other words, practice and skill are the key to fine cooking. In years past, before the days when aeroplanes and supermarkets blurred the seasons, the Chinese chef would have to apply all that practice and skill to only three or four main ingredients at a time. As cabbages or crabs came on stream, they would be subjected to countless subtle variations in the kitchen. In reality, most of the recipes are quite simple, but it's the simplicity of art.

The art of the Chinese cook is not only applied to the flavour of the food but also to the texture, colour and presentation. As for a painter or composer, balance and contrast are all-important. The crisp skin of a deep-fried duck is set off by the smoothness of boiled rice, the crunchiness of lightly cooked mange-tout peas by the softness of dumplings. Quick stir-frying keeps natural colours intact, so that your dish is lit up with the greens and reds and golds of spring onion, red pepper and sweetcorn. Fresh Chinese cabbage leaves make a picture with the pink of prawns. Slices of tomato and twists of lemon rind are thrown in just to add a dash of colour. Rice filling is wrapped in a lotus leaf and tied delicately with Chinese water-weed, like a Christmas gift for a lover!

Why then does your local Chinese takeaway not appear to be a temple of the culinary art? Why does it have hardly any Chinese customers? Actually, a lot of takeaways have very good cooks, producing fresh, tasty food to order. But the reason Chinese people don't like them much is that this food is not designed to go cold and soggy and be reheated in a microwave. Another proverb says, 'It is better for a man to wait for his meal than for a meal to wait for a man.' My advice is – eat it (almost) straight out of the wok or the steamer!

My next piece of advice is this: it may all look very enigmatic, but you too can come to grips with the mysteries of the East. Those chopsticks are perfectly easy to use if you hold the bowl up to your mouth in the Chinese manner. Get yourself some soya sauce, garlic, ginger and a wok: slice up the best raw materials you can get your hands on, and go for it. Now let me think… which proverb would be most appropriate? Perhaps: 'A journey of a thousand miles begins with a single step.'

Yung Yung Yum Yum Soup Dumplings

Serves 4–6

1 pack ready-made wonton skins or
for dough skins
350g (12oz) plain flour
2 eggs
600ml (1 pint) boiling water
5 tablespoons cold water

for the stuffing
110-150g (4-5oz) roast duck meat
110-150g (4-5oz) roast lean pork
50g (2oz) Chinese mushrooms
50g (2oz) cooked crabmeat
50g (2oz) shrimps
225g (8oz) Chinese white cabbage
1 teaspoon salt
1 tablespoon light soya sauce
1 teaspoon sugar
pinch of pepper
5 tablespoons vegetable oil

for the sauce
5 tablespoons red vinegar
2 tablespoons shredded fresh ginger
2 tablespoons soya sauce (optional)

additional ingredient for cooking the dumplings
clear chicken broth or fragrant Chinese soup

The method of sealing the dumplings has been simplified from the decorative and complicated traditional method at which Chinese chefs are adept. I have named this soup after my friend Yung Yung because she first introduced me to Yum Yum Soup at the New Emperor Restaurant in Manchester.

1 First make the dumpling skins, unless using ready-made, by sifting the flour into a bowl and mixing in the boiling water. Leave for 5 minutes. Add the cold water and knead well to form a dough. Set aside.

2 For the stuffing, prepare and assemble all your ingredients and mix well together in a bowl.

3 On a clean, lightly floured work surface form the dough into a long roll and then cut off 2.5cm (1in) pieces. Roll each piece into a flat pancake and then place a tablespoon of the stuffing in the centre. Brush all around the edges with water or beaten egg. Fold the pancake in half to form a half circle and seal the edges firmly together by pressing down on them with the prongs of a fork.

4 In a large ban on a low to medium flame bring the stock or soup to a simmer. Then add the dumplings and simmer for about 10 minutes.

5 Mix all the sauce ingredients together. Serve with the hot soup and dumplings and add spoonfuls of the sauce to individual servings of the soup for a delicious taste.

Tasty Tofu Triangles

2 large blocks of silk tofu
  approximately 15 x 10 x 2.5cm
  (6 x 4 x 1in) vegetable oil for deep
  frying in a wok

for the filling
4-6 shiitake mushrooms, blanched,
  drained and very finely chopped
1 carrot, peeled and very finely
  minced
100g (3^1/2oz) other vegetarian meat
  of your choice – such as duck,
  mince and chicken
2 tablespoons tapioca flour
salt and pepper to taste

for the sauce
savoury soy bean paste
water or sweet wine (optional)

This neat little trick with tofu is one of the many fun recipes I was taught by Mrs Kim Chan, the head chef at the Buddhist Temple in Manchester. Kim and her colleague, So Kwan, patiently taught me and I got so good that I taught Kok-Cheung Tang, one of the Chinese helpers, how to make them!

1 Place the tofu blocks on a chopping board and cut them into triangular blocks to make 16 triangles. Next carefully and gently cut out a small triangular piece from the centre of each small block to be stuffed. Save the pieces you cut out so they can be mashed and added to the stuffing.

2 Mix together all the filling ingredients, season to taste with salt and pepper and, using the tip of a blunt knife, carefully stuff the cut out holes of each tofu block with filling, taking care to pat and press down firmly so filling does not dislodge during frying. Once done, smooth the tops of the stuffing with the flat side of your knife. Repeat with the remaining tofu block. Arrange the stuffed tofu on a flat place.

3 Heat the oil in a wok and deep fry in small batches until golden – about 3–4 minutes. Remove and drain on crumpled kitchen paper. Blend the sauce ingredients together, heat to warm and pour over the stuffed tofu triangles to serve.

Tofu in Black Bean Sauce

Serves 4

2 packets fresh tofu
1 litre (1^3/4 pints) vegetable oil
2–3 cloves garlic, peeled and crushed
1 tablespoon dried black beans
1 chilli, deseeded and finely chopped
2 green peppers, deseeded and diced
2 small onions, peeled and diced
2 small carrots,
3 teaspoons soya sauce
1 teaspoon shaohing wine or sherry
1 teaspoon sesame oil
250ml (9fl oz) vegetable stock
1 teaspoon sugar and salt to taste
3 tablespoons cornflour, slaked in a
  little water

1 Slice each tofu block into four pieces and separate. Heat the vegetable oil in a wok and deep fry the tofu in batches until golden brown. Remove and drain on crumpled kitchen paper. Drain and wipe out the wok. Soak the beans in water for fifteen minutes and drain. Slice and blanch the carrots in boiling water for one minute.

2 Reheat the wok and add one tablespoon of vegetable oil. When hot add the garlic, black beans and chillies, and stir-fry, mashing the black beans against the side of the wok. Then add the green peppers, onions and carrots, stir-frying constantly and keeping the ingredients moving briskly around the pan

3 Add the soya sauce, wine and sesame oil. Stir and toss for one minute and then add the stock, sugar and salt to taste and bring to the boil. Reduce heat and add slaked cornflour to thicken, stirring constantly. Return the tofu and stir gently and reheat.

Salt & Pepper Chicken Wings

Serves 4

12 chicken wings
1 teaspoon salt.
6 tablespoons cornflour
1 litre (1³/4 pints) approximately vegetable oil
2 cloves garlic, peeled and crushed
2 medium red chillies, slit lengthways, deseeded and flesh finely chopped
1 small onion, peeled and diced
1 green pepper, deseeded and diced
¹/2 teaspoon Chinese Five-Spice powder
1–2 teaspoons sugar
1 teaspoon shaohing wine or sherry
1 teaspoon sesame oil

1 Wash chicken wings under running water, pat dry on kitchen paper and sprinkle with half the salt, the wine and the sesame oil to flavour. Prepare and assemble the remaining ingredients. Mix the remaining salt, the Five-Spice and the sugar in a small bowl.

2 Put the cornflour into a large polythene bag, add the chicken wings and shake to coat. Remove from bag, shaking off any excess cornflour.

3 Heat the vegetable oil in a large deep wok on a moderate flame and when hot deep-fry four chicken wings at a time in the gently bubbling oil for approximately three minutes, or until crisp and golden. Remove from oil with a slotted spoon and drain on crumpled kitchen paper.

4 Drain the oil from the wok, wipe out with kitchen paper and then return a tablespoon of vegetable oil. Heat again on a medium flame, then add garlic, chillies, onions and peppers and stir-fry briskly, keeping everything moving around the pan for one minute.

5 Return the chicken wings to the wok and toss with the vegetables. Sprinkle with the mixture of salt, sugar and Five-Spice while tossing, add the sesame oil and wine to season.

Fujian Fried Rice

Serves 4 as an accompaniment

450g (1lb) boiled rice – cooked weight
120g (4¹/2oz) pork, or chicken, shredded, uncooked
2 Chinese mushrooms, soaked, cleaned, stalks removed, shredded
225g (8oz) shelled prawns or chopped squid or shredded roast duck meat
³/4 tablespoon light soya sauce
splash of rice wine or dry sherry
asparagus, bamboo shoot, spring onion, chopped in small pieces
1 tablespoon vegetable oil

This original recipe is from the Fujian Province of China. It has several names – each difficult to pronounce like: Fuchian, Fukien, Fukian. The correct pronunciation is 'Foo-kee-en'. Linda and Yung Yung thought I created quite a stir at the New Emperor Restaurant when I tried to pronounce the name. Whatever the name is, it tastes great!

1 Clean and wash the prawns (or squid). Prepare and assemble remaining ingredients. Season the pork (or chicken) with the light soya sauce and rice wine or sherry.

2 Heat a wok over a medium flame and when hot add the vegetable oil. Stir-fry the Chinese mushrooms until the fragrance comes out and then add the pork or chicken shreds and stir-fry until they start taking colour.

3 Add all the remaining ingredients and continue to stir-fry for one minute. Add the rice and toss and stir-fry until heated through. Serve immediately with the chicken wings.

Assorted Vegetables
in Spicy Coconut Sauce

275g (10oz) broccoli, cut in florets
275g (10oz) mangetout peas, cleaned
    and trimmed
275g (10oz) baby corn, cut in small
    pieces
275g (10oz) straw mushrooms
1 tablespoon vegetable oil
1 egg yolk
1/2 bottle Portuguese Spicy Coconut
    Sauce, available at specialist Asian
    food stores
salt and a sprinkle of sugar to taste

for the sauce
1 1/2 tablespoons curry sauce
50g (2oz) butter
110g (4oz) plain flour
2 tablespoons evaporated milk
2 tablespoons coconut sauce
480ml (18fl oz) water

The beauty of this dish is that there is no restriction on what vegetables to put in. Choose four different types. The ingredients given here are one suggested mixture.

This seemed a rather unusual dish for a Chinese restaurant – what with the mixture of coconut and curry sauce mixed with baby corn and other vegetables, so I asked for the recipe. This dish goes very well with Fujian Fried rice (see page 52) or with plain Fried Rice (see page 54).

1 First prepare and assemble all the ingredients. Pre-heat the oven to its highest setting.

2 Now make the sauce. Melt the butter in a heavy-based pan over a medium heat and stir in the flour to make a smooth roux. Gradually add the milk and water and bring to a gentle simmer to produce a thick sauce. Add the coconut sauce and curry sauce and stir well to produce a golden-brown colour. Set aside.

3 Heat the wok, and when hot add the vegetable oil. Stir-fry all the vegetables briskly, keeping everything moving around the pan. Add the water and salt to taste, bring back to simmer and transfer to a baking casserole.

4 Bring the spicy coconut sauce back to the boil, add the evaporated milk and egg yolk, stirring well. Pour over the assorted vegetables.

5 Put into the pre-heated oven and bake until golden brown – about 10 minutes.

Dorinda's Special Stir-Fry

Serves 4

2 sliced chicken breast fillets
  (steamed in a little chicken stock,
  flavoured with 2 teaspoons sherry
  and 1 teaspoon sesame oil for 5
  minutes)
200g (6oz) unshelled king prawns
3 tablespoons vegetable oil
1cm (½in) fresh ginger, peeled and
  sliced into three
2 cloves garlic, crushed and peeled
110g (4oz) broccoli, cut in florets
  and blanched
50g (2oz) mange tout peas
50g (2oz) straw mushrooms
50g (2oz) baby sweetcorn, chopped
  in bite-size pieces
1 small onion, diced
½ green pepper, diced
1 red chilli, slit lengthways, deseeded
  and flesh finely chopped
250ml (9fl oz) chicken stock
2 tablespoons shaohing wine or
  sherry
1 teaspoon sesame oil
2 teaspoons soya sauce
1 teaspoon salt, to taste

Created by Kin Man Lee and me in his take-away shop, The Oriental Express; it was the first time I had cooked with an industrial size wok and in a commercial kitchen so I concocted this recipe with his supervision and gained high praise ... when he tasted it.

1 Cut the drained and cooled chicken slices into thin strips. Prepare and assemble all other ingredients. (The secret of stir-frying is to have every ingredient ready in advance and to work quickly so that ingredients cook but keep their crispness.)

2 Heat a wok dry on a medium flame, then add vegetable oil when hot. Add ginger slices, stir until browned, then add the chopped garlic. Cook for half a minute.

3 Add the broccoli, mange tout, mushrooms and corn and stir-fry briskly. Stir in the king prawns and chicken pieces, then add the onions, green peppers and chilli, adding more oil around the edge of the wok, if necessary, to stop ingredients sticking.

4 Stir-fry for 1–1½ minutes then add the stock, wine, sesame oil, and soya sauce, stirring constantly. Add salt to taste, bearing in mind that the soya sauce is very salty.

5 Now add the slaked cornflour, stirring all the time. Simmer for ½ minute to thicken. Serve with plain boiled rice or with Fried Rice.

Fried Rice

Serves 4

900g (2lb) cooked rice, cooked
  weight
2–3 tablespoons vegetable oil
2 eggs, preferably free range, lightly
  beaten
2 tablespoons soya sauce
1 teaspoon sesame oil
salt to taste

Invest in the best wok you can afford and cook the rice freshly.

1 First heat the wok on a medium flame and, when it is hot, add the vegetable oil, and swirl around the pan.

2 When the oil is hot, pour in the beaten eggs and stir all around the wok two or three times, then leave it to cook for a minute or two, until the egg is set.

3 Tip in the rice, stir-fry and scramble it with the egg until evenly mixed and heated through. Add a dash or two of soya sauce, whilst stir-frying continuously.

4 Sprinkle on salt to taste, bearing in mind that the soya sauce is salty, and season with sesame oil. Serve immediately.

Sautéed Chicken
with Small Onions and Black Bean Sauce

Serves 2

275g (10oz) chicken breast, cut in
  bite sized pieces
1 tablespoon vegetable oil
1 cm (1/2in) ginger, peeled and
  sliced in four
3 spring onions, trimmed and chopped
  in lengths, green part included
1 tablespoon wine
2 tablespoons soya sauce
6–8 baby onions, peeled
1 green pepper, deseeded and
  chopped
75ml (3fl oz) water
4 tablespoons dried black beans,
  soaked until soft and then drained
  or commercial variety of black bean
  sauce on sale in most supermarkets
  salt and freshly ground black pepper

Like most Chinese recipes, the preparation takes longer than the cooking. But then, in this dish all the ingredients are readily available.

1 Prepare and assemble all the ingredients.

2 Heat a wok over a medium flame and pour in the oil when hot. Add the spring onion and ginger slices and stir-fry. Sprinkle in the wine and soya sauce.

3 Add the chicken pieces, baby onions and chopped green pepper. Stir-fry briskly, keeping everything moving around the pan.

4 Now add the water and black beans, season to taste, stir well, cover and simmer until cooked – about 5–7 minutes.

Gongbao Chicken

Serves 2

350g (12oz) chicken breast, cut in
  1–1.5cm (1/2–3/4in) dice
1 carrot, peeled and cut in 1–1.5cm
  (1/2–3/4in) dice
50g (2oz) peanuts
15g (1/2oz) spring onion, trimmed
  and sliced
15g (1/2oz) garlic, peeled and
  chopped
6 tablespoons vegetable oil
2 teaspoons whole dried chillies
powder
salt to taste
15g (1/2oz) sugar
2 tablespoons soya sauce
15g (1/2oz) vinegar
25g (1oz) cornflour
pinch gourmet powder

Lauren X. B. Lee is from Szechwan and says she loves cooking Gongbao Chicken, a spicy Szechwan dish, typical of the region and Lauren says it evokes memories of home. Adjust the chillies to suit your taste buds ...

1 First prepare and assemble all the ingredients. In a bowl mix the soya sauce, vinegar, sugar, gourmet powder and cornflour and add water to make the sauce to thicken the dish.

2 Heat the work, then add the vegetable oil when it is hot and swirl the oil round to coat the pan. When the oil is hot add the dried chillies and stir-fry until it goes brown. Then put in the chicken and stir-fry again.

3 When the chicken is cooked, about 2 minutes, add the carrot, ginger, spring onion and garlic. Stir-fry again, moving the ingredients briskly around the pan.

4 Now add the sauce mixture and stir through until it thickens and is hot. Finally add the peanuts, stir again quickly and serve on a warmed dish.

Shallow-fried Whole Sea Bass

Serves 2–3 (with other dishes)

Sea bass weighing 500–750g
  (1–1¼lb)
vegetable oil for frying
2 or 3 sprigs coriander for
  garnish

for the sauce
1 teaspoon ginger, peeled and finely
  chopped
1½ teaspoons spring onions,
  chopped
light soya sauce
½ teaspoon sugar
250ml (8fl oz) fish stock
1 teaspoon sugar

1 Scale and gut the fish, rinse under cold running water and pat dry with kitchen paper.

2 Heat the wok with a dessertspoonful of pure vegetable oil. Make sure the oil is hot, add a pinch of salt and place the fish in the wok. The heat will grill the fish, sealing in the flavour. Turn down the heat slightly and cook for about four minutes. Turn the fish and cook for a further four minutes. Remove to a warm dish and keep warm.

3 Make the sauce. Reheat the wok with another dessertspoonful of oil. Add the sugar and the ginger. The sugar will quickly caramelise. Then add a dessertspoon of soya sauce and the fish stock.

4 Put the fish back in the wok and cook for about three minutes, turning once. Add the spring onion and cook for a further 10–12 seconds before removing the fish and putting on a heated serving plate. Pour the sauce from the wok over the fish and garnish with the sprigs of coriander.

Braised Pak Choi
with Beancurd & Chinese Mushrooms

Serves 2–3 (with other dishes)

300g (12oz) small Pak Choi
200g (8oz) beancurd
10–12 dried shiitake mushrooms
1 slice ginger, peeled
1 spring onion, washed and trimmed
chicken stock

for the sauce
oyster sauce
salt
sugar
chicken powder
potato starch or cornflour

1 Wash the pak choi. Soak the mushrooms in hot water for two hours, then remove from the bowl and remove and discard any stems. Place the mushrooms in a steamer and add the ginger and spring onion and steam till tender. Alternatively, buy tinned shiitake mushrooms, but obviously the taste will be different.

2 Meanwhile cut the beancurd into rectangles roughly 1cm x 1cm x 2.5cm (½in x ½in x 1in) and deep fry in very hot oil for three to four minutes.

3 Put the chicken stock into a wok and heat to boiling point, then add the pak choi and boil for about two minutes. Drain the stock, keeping the pak choi in the wok, add a teaspoon of oil and stir fry for about one minute.

4 Remove the pak choi from the wok and arrange on the serving dish. Keep warm.

5 Put 250–300ml (8–10fl oz) of chicken stock into the wok, add the beancurd and mushrooms together with a pinch each of salt and sugar. Add a dessertspoon of oyster sauce and half a teaspoon of chicken powder. Cook for two or three minutes. Thicken with a teaspoon of potato starch or cornflour, slaked with a few drops of water.

6 Arrange the beancurd on top of the pak choi and then put the mushrooms on top of the beancurd and pour over the sauce.

Glutinous Rice Parcel

Serves 3–4 (with other dishes)

Start preparation two days in advance of the proposed meal.

110g (4oz) split green beans
110g (4oz) pork fat
Five-Spice powder
pinch of salt
1 teaspoonful rice wine
110g (4oz) glutinous rice
pure vegetable oil
1 large lotus leaf
5 or 6 bamboo leaves
1 dried shiitake mushroom, soaked in
    warm water for 2 hours
2 or 3 chestnuts
1 slice of breast of duck
1 slice crispy belly pork
4 or 5 small diced shrimps
1 salted duck egg yolk

Centuries ago, a revered local Chinese hero was exiled by political enemies. Anguished at the thought of never returning home, he drowned himself in the river. The townsfolk were distraught and so they threw rice parcels into the water to stop the fish eating his remains. It has become tradition to throw them into the river during Rice Boat races.

1 Wash the green beans and soak in water overnight.

2 Marinate the pork fat in a bowl with a pinch each of salt and Five-Spice powder and rice wine. Leave overnight. The next day wash and drain the rice, place in a bowl and add a pinch of salt and a few drops of vegetable oil.

3 Take the lotus leaf and lay it out fully on a work surface and cover with the bamboo leaves so they overlap each other. When you seal the parcel they act as an inner lining.

4 Place the mushroom in the centre of the flattened-out parcel and then add half the rice and half the split green beans on top of the rice. Place all the other ingredients on top and then cover with the rest of the green beans and the rice.

5 This is the delicate part. Wrap the lotus leaf like a Xmas parcel for your beloved, folding the side into the centre. Tie the parcel with string. Traditionally you should use Chinese water weed to tie the parcel, but string will do!

6 Totally submerge the parcel in a pan of water and bring to the boil, allowing to simmer for 4½ hours, adding water when necessary to keep the parcel submerged.

7 Leave to cool and soak in the water for twelve hours, then remove and keep in the fridge until required. When you are ready to serve your meal, replace in a pan of hot water, bring to the boil and cook for 20 minutes. Drain, remove the lotus and bamboo leaves, which should be discarded, place the rice parcels in a dish and serve. Have two small bowls, one of sugar and one of soya sauce so that your guests can add to taste.

Sweet Rice Parcels

Makes 6 rice parcels

600g (1⅓lb) glutinous rice
2 teaspoons lye – optional (available
  from Chinese supermarkets)
4 teaspoons vegetable oil
350g (12oz) lotus seed mash
225g (8oz) dumpling leaves
  available from Chinese
  supermarkets
wrapping straw

for the syrup

225g (8oz) granulated sugar
3 tablespoons maltase
4 tablespoons water

1 Wash rice under cold running water, then soak in cold water in a large bowl for two hours. Drain and return to the bowl, add lye (if used) and vegetable oil, mixing well. Cover bowl with a wet cloth and leave for three hours.

2 Meanwhile soak dumpling leaves for 30 minutes, then simmer in boiling water for 10 minutes. Drain well and set aside. Wash the wrapping straw.

3 On a clean working surface place one piece of dumpling leaf on top of another and cross the two ends to form a hollow in the middle. Put in a layer of glutinous rice and some lotus seed mash and cover with another layer of glutinous rice. Fold edges of dumpling leaves inward. Holding tight to the centre of the dumpling, trim the hard tissue off the leaf and fold the two sides of the leaves inwards. Work into a rectangular shape. Wrap the two ends with straw and tie knots to secure. Cut away excess straw. Do not tie the dumplings too tight.

4 Transfer the dumplings to a large heavy-based pan with enough boiling water to cover the dumplings. Cover and cook over a high flame for 2½ hours, topping up with boiling water if necessary. Remove from heat and set aside for a further 2 hours, keeping the lid on.

5 To make the syrup put all the ingredients into a wok and cook over a low heat until it begins to take on a slightly yellow appearance. Remove from heat immediately, otherwise the syrup will quickly become brown and caramelised.

6 Serve the Sweet Rice Parcels with the syrup or with granulated sugar.

Snowballs

Makes 14–18

275g (10oz) glutinous rice flour
hot water to mix
40g (1½oz) fine flaked coconut
1 tablespoon vegetable oil

1 Put glutinous rice flour in a bowl and mix in the tablespoon of oil. Gradually add hot water, stirring all the time with a wooden spoon to make a softish dough. Knead dough until smooth and resilient, adding more rice flour if the dough is too sticky.

2 Divide dough into small portions, press flat and then work into balls table-tennis–ball size.

3 Arrange the dough balls on a plate and steam for five minutes. Remove from steamer. Sprinkle with the coconut, making sure the whole ball is covered. Serve hot.

Chapter 4: Pakistani

The British love affair with the Indian sub-continent goes back a long way – to the days of the Raj and beyond. But until quite recently there were very few Asian people and even fewer Asian foods in Britain. When I was first in London more than 30 years ago, you could get mango chutney, Sharwood's curry powder, mulligatawny soup in tins – and that was about it!

In fact that was about the time when the great Indian restaurant revolution was taking off. Now we can hardly remember a time when going out for an Indian meal wasn't as much a part of British life as complaining about the weather. Now, for two million people a week, it is more a part of life than fish and chips.

In the late fifties and early sixties, with labour shortages in Britain, and Commonwealth citizens having the right to live here, lots of men from certain parts of the sub-continent came to work. Their plan was to earn enough and then go home. They left the women behind, at a safe distance from the corrupting influence of modern English life. Later the women realised that while they themselves were 'safe' from corruption, their menfolk weren't! Anyway, of course, families needed to be reunited, and so wives and daughters came to Britain too. And that's when the restaurant boom began.

But surely (you are thinking) the restaurants are run by men. That's true, but you can bet the men didn't cook the family's meals every day in the Punjab or Bengal! The whole food culture belonged to the women, and once they were here they could transmit it to their husbands and sons in the catering business. Even today some chefs phone home to get a bit of advice, or inspiration when they run out of ideas.

We've been calling them Indian restaurants, but in fact most of them are Pakistani or Bangladeshi. Bangladesh used to be part of Pakistan, until the civil war in 1972; and Pakistan used to be part of 'India', until partition in 1947. There are language and religious communities which straddle borders all over the place. Mirpur, where most of the Asians In Bradford originate, is part of Kashmir – which is a territory disputed by India and Pakistan. It's all far from straightforward... so let's talk about food, which unites rather than divides the human race! The first mystery to be explained is why Pakistani and Bangladeshi restaurants all tend to have the same menus. Where are all the regional cuisines? An important factor for Britain is that much of that regional

Making gelabie – a lot harder than it looks, but the taste makes it worthwhile.

With Mumtaz and the best mango lassi in the world – and I've tasted a lot.

cuisine is vegetarian (very much a minority taste until recently), whereas they are great meat-eaters in Pakistan. But I was amazed when someone told me that you find the same lack of choice in restaurants in India! Since the businessmen who travel around the sub-continent are mostly Punjabi, and restaurant customers are mostly businessmen, restaurant food is mostly Punjabi. After all, people don't go out to a restaurant to eat things that they cook better at home.

This strange fact also lies at the heart of the image problem that Indian/Pakistani restaurants are suffering from right now. Not only do most menus look the same, most of the food actually tastes the same, too. But following my recent travels around Britain, in particular Yorkshire and the West Midlands, I'm convinced that things are all set to change, and that in a few years' time you will be able to enjoy a massive range of really fresh and different regional dishes in a restaurant near you. Why, I even sat in on Mohammed Aslam's version of *Can't Cook Won't Cook*, teaching locals in Garforth how to make tasty, spicy Pakistani meals like those on offer at his Aagrah Restaurant. In the meantime, get into the kitchen with this book open on the next few pages and try it for yourself!

Pakora

Makes about 24 pakora

for the batter
225g (8oz) gram (chickpea) flour, approximately
1/3 teaspoon bicarbonate of soda
1 1/2 teaspoons salt, to taste
1–2 teaspoons red chilli powder, to taste
1 1/2 teaspoons dried pomegranate seed (optional)
300ml (1/2 pint) water, approximately

for the vegetables
150g (5oz) cauliflower, washed and cut in florets 3.5cm (1 1/2in)
1 medium potato, peeled, cut in half lengthways and thinly sliced
1 medium onion, peeled, cut in half lengthways and thinly sliced
1 small aubergine, washed and thinly sliced
75g (3oz) fresh spinach leaves, washed and roughly chopped
4 green chillies, slit lengthways, deseeded and flesh chopped

for deep frying
vegetable oil

to serve
Green Chutney (see page 66)

Asian cooking uses lots of garlic, often puréd. The easiest way to prepare the cloves is to paste them on to a board. Use the flat of a kitchen knife to crush the unpeeled cloves and the papery skin can then be removed easily. Chop, mince or hash the crushed cloves. Then slant the knife blade and work the garlic into a paste or coarse purée with a pinch or two of salt. This is a quick and satisfying process, used by professional chefs for preparing garlic and root ginger.

Pakora, a snack of vegetable fritters, is made in some shape or size across the length and breadth of the sub-continent. Pakora is a Punjabi or Urdu word, which is generally known as Bhajjia in India. Throughout Europe it is known as 'onion Bhaji' which totally misrepresents the actual snack, Pakora. Pakora and Bhajjia must consist of several vegetables at least, and the recipe below is for an assorted vegetable pakora. Mumtaz's method for the Pakora, learned from his mother in the family kitchen, is a quick and instinctive way of bypassing making a batter as a separate step.

For advance preparation for a party, prepare and half-fry the pakora, drain and set aside. When ready to serve them hot and fresh, it is a simple procedure to deep-fry them for 2 minutes to complete their cooking time.

1 Put all the ingredients for the batter, except for the water, into a very large mixing bowl. Add all the prepared vegetables and use your hands to begin tossing them through the dry batter mixture.

2 Now start adding a splash or two of water (3–4 tablespoons), working through the vegetables and batter mixture with your other hand as you go. Keep adding a splash or two of water until gradually a batter forms and adheres to the mixed vegetables. It is easy to get a feel for the correct consistency as you work with this very quick and instinctive method.

3 In a suitable pan for deep-frying, heat the vegetable oil to smoking point. Take heaped tablespoons of the combined mixed vegetables and slide them one by one into the hot oil. (If you find that the vegetables are separating whilst frying, add a little more gram flour into the mix.) Deep-fry them for 3–5 minutes, until golden brown. Do not overcrowd the pan – you will probably need to fry them in two or three batches. Use a perforated spoon to lift out the pakora and drain on kitchen paper.

4 Serve hot, with Green Chutney (see page 66).

Spiced Dal

Depending on how much water you add, dal can be served as a soup or a main course.

Serves 4

Ingredients
350g (12oz) split peas
2 tomatoes, peeled and chopped
1.4 litres (2½ pints) water
1 teaspoon salt, to taste
1½ tablespoons vegetable oil
3–4 cloves garlic, crushed, peeled and finely chopped to a purée
1 teaspoon mustard seed
1 teaspoon garam masala powder
1 teaspoon red chilli powder
1 teaspoon coriander seed, ground

to finish
handful of fresh coriander leaves

1 Put the split peas into a sieve and rinse under running water. Put the split peas and chopped tomatoes into a medium-sized heavy-based pan with the water, bring to the boil, turn the heat to a low flame and simmer with the pan partly covered until the peas are tender and almost mushy – about 1 hour. Add the salt at the end of the cooking time. Remove from the heat, cool slightly, then put the peas into the bowl of a liquidiser or blender and pulse to a fine purée. Set aside.

2 Wash the pan, reheat over a low to moderate flame, add the oil and, when hot, put in the garlic and mustard seeds. As the seeds begin to pop (about 30 seconds) add all the remaining spices, stir once or twice, then immediately add the split pea purée to the pan, stirring well to amalgamate. Continue to cook for 3–4 minutes. If wished, more water may be added to adjust the consistency to serve the dal as a soup.

3 Pour the dal into a warmed serving bowl and scatter over the roughly chopped coriander leaves.

Green Chutney

This dip goes with just about everything!

225g (8oz) fresh coriander leaves
225g (8oz) fresh mint leaves
50g (2oz) onion, finely chopped
4 green chillies, slit lengthways, deseeded and flesh finely chopped
2 tablespoons desiccated coconut
pinch of salt to taste
400g (14oz) natural yoghurt

to finish
whole leaves of fresh coriander and mint

1 Put all the ingredients into the bowl of a blender or liquidiser and pulse to a fine paste. You may have to pause once or twice and use a rubber spatula to push the ingredients back down to the blades.

2 Tip the Green Chutney into an attractive bowl, sprinkle over a few of the reserved coriander and mint leaves, and serve as a dip with snacks or as an accompaniment to a main course.

Prawn Pilau

Serves 4–6

450g (1lb) basmati rice

For the aromatic stock
1 litre (1³/4 pints) water
4 cardamoms, crushed
15cm (6in) piece cinnamon stick
8–10 whole bay leaves

For the prawns and spices
*450g (1lb) shelled prawns, rinsed if
    fresh, defrosted if frozen*
2 tablespoons vegetable ghee
*1 medium onion, peeled and
    chopped*
*4 cloves garlic, crushed, peeled and
    roughly chopped*
*2.5cm (1in) piece root ginger, peeled
    and finely chopped to a purée*
*4 green chillies, slit lengthways,
    deseeded and flesh finely chopped*
1¹/2 tablespoons whole cumin seed
2 teaspoons ground black pepper
3 teaspoons ground coriander seed
2–3 teaspoons salt, to taste

to finish
*sprigs of coriander and slices of lime
    (optional)*

**This dish is tasty yet easy to prepare and turns an ordinary rice cook
into a cordon bleu one.**

1 Preheat the oven to 190°C/375°F/gas mark 5.

2 First put the rice into a roomy sieve and rinse it thoroughly under running water.
Tip the rice into a large basin and leave it to soak in plenty of warm water for 20–30
minutes. Then drain the rice back into the sieve and leave it to stand.

3 Meanwhile, bring the water to the boil in a large pan and add the cardamom,
cinnamon sticks and bay leaves. Simmer briskly for 10–15 minutes to produce a light
aromatic stock. Set aside and leave to further infuse.

4 Spread the prawns on a plate of crumpled kitchen paper to drain and pat dry.

5 Now, using a largish heavy-based pan which is also lidded and ovenproof, heat the
ghee over a medium flame. Slide in the chopped onions and fry them with care,
stirring from time to time, for at least 10 minutes or until they are dark golden brown
but not at all burned.

6 Add the garlic, ginger, chillies, prawns and whole cumin seed and continue stir-
frying for 2 minutes.

7 Keep stirring and add the black pepper, coriander seed, salt and cook for a further
minute. Pour in the strained aromatic broth and bring to the boil.

8 Now tip in the drained rice and, on a medium heat, stir gently from time to time to
combine all the ingredients and cook until the rice has absorbed all the liquid. This
will take about 10 minutes. Don't allow the dish to become too dry.

9 Cover with a tight-fitting lid and cook in the pre-heated oven for 20 minutes. Turn
out the pilau, fluffing it up with a fork, onto a warmed serving platter and garnish
with sprigs of coriander and slices of lime.

Goan Chilli King Prawns

Serves 4

*900g (2lb) uncooked, unpeeled
medium-sized king prawns
400g (14oz) tin coconut milk*

for the ground spices
*5–10 green chillies to taste, slit
lengthways, deseeded and flesh
finely chopped
1 teaspoon turmeric powder
1 teaspoon freshly ground black
pepper
1½ tablespoons coriander seed
and1½ teaspoons cumin seed all
ground together
1¼ tablespoons white poppy seed
2 tablespoons vegetable oil
2 medium onions, peeled, halved
and sliced into fine half rings
2 cloves garlic, peeled and sliced into
fine slivers
1cm (½in) piece root ginger, peeled
and sliced into fine slivers
3 teaspoons tamarind paste (if
unobtainable, use a squeeze or
two of fresh lemon juice)
pinch of salt to taste
120ml (scant ¼ pint) water
2 tablespoons fresh coriander leaves,
roughly chopped*

to serve
*reserved fresh coriander leaves,
chopped*

TIP: Before you start cooking
Pakistani or Indian style, take a
trip down to a well-stocked
Asian grocery store with your
recipes and stock up on a few
of the more unusual spices
because you will be using them
throughout this chapter and
beyond.

Not everybody likes peeling saucy prawns at the dinner table so an alternative method with this dish is to peel and 'butterfly' the prawns before using in recipe or buy ones already peeled and butterflied by the fishmonger. However, it is worth remembering that the shells add extra flavour to the dish. For the final effect when serving, garnish with lots of freshly chopped coriander leaves.

1 For the preparation before cooking the dish, rinse the uncooked, unpeeled prawns under running water, pat dry with kitchen paper and set aside. Open the tin of coconut milk, taking care not to shake or disturb the contents. Use a spoon to scoop out the settled cream in the top part of the tin, transfer this cream into a small bowl and set aside. Now top up the tin containing the remaining thin coconut milk with water, put in a bowl and set aside.

2 To prepare the spice paste, put the chopped chillies, turmeric, freshly ground black pepper, coriander seed, cumin seed and 4 tablespoons of the thin coconut milk into the bowl of a blender or liquidiser, grind to a paste and pour this paste back into the bowl of thin coconut milk. Grind the white poppy seed in a coffee grinder and add these also to the spicy coconut milk mixture.

3 Now heat the oil in a large heavy-based pan on a medium flame, add the onions, garlic and ginger and stir-fry until the onions are golden-brown at the edges.

4 Pour in the spicy coconut milk mixture, add the tamarind paste or lemon juice, a pinch of salt to taste, the 120ml (scant ¼ pint) water and the chopped coriander leaves. Turn the heat down, cover the pan and simmer gently for 10 minutes.

5 Finally add the king prawns with the reserved thick coconut cream, stir and bring the dish back to simmer gently until the prawns turn opaque and are cooked through.

6 Spoon the finished dish into a warmed serving dish and sprinkle with the reserved coriander leaves and serve with rice.

Fish Masala

Serves 4

Begin marinating at least 4 hours ahead, or overnight

450g (1lb) cod, haddock, coley or other firm white fish fillets

for the marinade
1½ tablespoons mustard or vegetable oil
½ tablespoon each of cumin seed and coriander seed, ground together
1½ teaspoons salt, to taste
1½ teaspoons turmeric powder
3 teaspoons gram (chickpea) flour
3 teaspoons ajowan seed (if unobtainable, try lovage or celery seed)
3 cloves garlic, crushed, peeled and finely chopped to a purée

for frying
vegetable oil

It is well worth having the correct spices for this dish to get the authentic taste.

1 First prepare the fish, at least 4 hours in advance or the day before you are ready to cook. Check for bones; skin and trim if necessary and cut into four pieces. Rinse in salted water and leave in a colander to drain.

2 Mix together the marinade ingredients in a small bowl. This makes quite a thick paste. If the mixture feels too stiff, stir in a little more oil.

3 Smother this paste all over the pieces of fish, put them into a shallow dish, cover with clingfilm and leave in a cool place or the refrigerator to marinate for a minimum of 4 hours or overnight. This spicy paste will also act as a protective coating when deep-frying the fish.

4 In a pan suitable for deep-frying, heat the vegetable oil to just under smoking point. Lower the pieces of coated fish into the hot oil and fry for 8–12 minutes. Remove with a slotted spoon and drain on crumpled kitchen paper. The fish will have a deliciously spicy crispy coating, with succulent flakes of fish inside.

5 Serve on a warmed serving dish, with a selection of chutneys, a crisp green salad, and wedges of lemon.

Chicken Balti

Allow a minimum of 6 hours, or overnight, for marinating

Serves 4

900g (2lb) chicken, skinned, boned and cut into 2.5cm (1in) pieces

for the marinade
1 tablespoon vegetable oil
1 teaspoon salt
1 teaspoon red chilli powder
1 tablespoon coriander seed and 1 tablespoon cumin seed, ground together
2.5cm (1in) piece root ginger, peeled and very finely chopped or puréed
2 tablespoons lemon juice
3 teaspoons Tandoori Masala
1½ teaspoons ajowan seed, ground (if unobtainable, try lovage or celery seed)
3 tablespoons natural yoghurt

for cooking the chicken
2 tablespoons vegetable oil
4 cloves garlic, crushed, peeled and roughly chopped
1cm (½in) piece root ginger, peeled and very finely chopped or puréed
1½ teaspoons coriander seed and 1½ teaspoons cumin seed ground together
1½ teaspoons red chilli powder
1½teaspoons salt
¾ teaspoon turmeric powder

to finish
3 tomatoes
2 green chillies, slit lengthways, deseeded and flesh finely chopped
1 handful fresh coriander leaves, roughly chopped

additional preparation
metal skewers or pre-soaked wooden skewers

A very popular meal which until recently, was only known in Birmingham. Not so now: it's all the rage. The recipe gets its name from the dish in which it is cooked – a balti or a karahi – a two-handled pan which looks like a wok. (Balti curries are drier, and aromatic with plenty of herbs and are often served with Naan (see page 75) or other flat breads. They originated from Kashmir or the northern region of Pakistan.) A balti meal is one-pot cooking at its tasty best.

1 Begin by preparing the chicken for marinade. First wash the chicken pieces, pat dry with kitchen paper and set aside. Assemble, prepare and measure the spices for the marinade. (Since many of the spices are repeated in the cooking of the chicken, look at the list of total ingredients required and prepare simultaneously). Dry-roast the coriander and cumin seeds in a heavy-based frying pan. Grind these spices in a blender or food processor, then assemble the remaining marinade ingredients.

2 In a large non-metallic basin mix together the marinade ingredients, add the chicken and use your hands to combine thoroughly. Cover the dish with clingfilm and leave in a cool place or in the refrigerator for at least 6 hours or overnight.

3 When you are ready to cook, assemble all the remaining ingredients and spices. Thread the marinated chicken pieces onto metal or pre-soaked wooden skewers.

4 Pre-heat a grill, chargrill or ridged grill pan to hot. Cook batches of the skewered chicken for 4–5 minutes. Turn frequently to seal and sear. Aim for half-cooked chicken: the flesh should feel bouncy when pressed with your finger. Set aside.

5 Heat the oil in a large heavy-based pan on a medium heat, add the garlic and stir-fry for about 1 minute. Then add the ginger and the chicken: slide the pieces from their skewers straight into the pan. Stir for 1–2 minutes.

6 Now add the ground coriander and cumin seed, red chilli powder, salt and turmeric powder and continue to stir-fry for a few more minutes. Add the tomatoes and green chillies and cook for a further 5 minutes.

7 To finish the dish, stir in the fresh coriander, turn the Chicken Balti into a warmed serving dish and serve with rice or Naan Bread.

Chicken Tikka Masala

Allow a minimum of 6 hours, or overnight, for marinating

Serves 4

700g (1½lb) chicken breasts, skinned, boned and cut into 2.5cm (1in) pieces

for the marinade
4–5 tablespoons natural yoghurt
1 clove garlic, crushed, peeled and finely chopped to a purée
2.5cm (1in) piece root ginger, peeled and finely chopped or puréed
1 teaspoon salt, to taste
½ teaspoon red chilli powder, 1 each coriander seed and cumin seed, ground together
1 teaspoon garam masala powder
2 tablespoons tandoori masala powder
1 teaspoon lemon juice

for the masala
3–4 tablespoons vegetable oil
4 medium onions, chopped
2.5cm (1in) piece cinnamon stick
1 tablespoon cumin seed
3 black cardamom, pods removed
3 green cardamom, pods removed
4 cloves, crushed
4 peppercorns, crushed
2 bay leaves, broken and crushed
3 cloves garlic, crushed
3cm (1½in) piece root ginger, peeled and finely chopped to a purée
½–1 teaspoon red chilli powder
1 tablespoon coriander seed, crushed
½ teaspoon turmeric powder
½–1 teaspoon salt, to taste
5 tomatoes, peeled and quartered

to finish
4 green chillies, slit lengthways, deseeded and flesh finely chopped
handful fresh coriander leaves, roughly chopped

additional preparation
metal skewers or pre-soaked wooden skewers

1 Begin by preparing the chicken for marinade. First wash the chicken pieces, pat dry with kitchen paper and set aside. Assemble, prepare and measure the spices for the marinade. (Since many of the spices are repeated in the cooking of the chicken, look at the list of total ingredients required and prepare simultaneously). Dry-roast the coriander and cumin seeds in a heavy-based frying pan. Grind these spices in a blender or food processor, then assemble the remaining marinade ingredients.

2 In a large non-metallic basin mix together the marinade ingredients, add the chicken and use your hands to combine thoroughly. Cover the dish with clingfilm and leave in a cool place or in the refrigerator for at least 6 hours or overnight.

3 When you are ready to cook, assemble all the remaining ingredients and spices. Thread the marinated chicken pieces onto metal or pre-soaked wooden skewers.

4 Pre-heat a grill, chargrill or ridged grill pan to hot. Cook batches of the skewered chicken for 4–5 minutes. Turn frequently to seal and sear. Aim for half-cooked chicken; the flesh should feel bouncy when pressed with your finger. Set aside.

5 Heat the oil in a large heavy-based pan on a medium heat, add the onions and fry until they begin to soften, then add the cumin seed, black and green cardamom seeds, cloves, peppercorns and bay leaves. Stir-fry for a minute or two until the onions are pale golden, then add the garlic and ginger and continue frying for a further minute.

6 When the onions are a deep golden brown, add the red chilli powder, coriander seed, turmeric, salt, tomatoes and a splash or two of water.

7 Now add the chicken: slide the pieces from their skewers straight into the pan. Stir for 3–4 minutes.

8 To finish the dish, stir in the chopped green chillies and fresh coriander leaves. Spoon the Chicken Tikka Masala into a warmed serving dish and serve straight away with the Naan Bread (see opposite).

Naan Bread

900g (2lb) self-raising flour
1 teaspoon salt
2 tablespoons sesame seed
1 tablespoon onion seed
2 medium eggs
25g (1oz) dried yeast
150ml (¼ pint) tepid milk or water,
  approximately

Naan comes in different varieties – plain, garlic, spinach, lentil, even cheese. They are the favoured accompaniment to curries in northern regions of India whilst the southern regions prefer rice. This is a basic Naan recipe which you can make as exciting as you choose.

1 Put all the dry ingredients into a large mixing bowl, using your fingers to combine. Gradually pour in the tepid milk or water, mixing all the time with your free hand, drawing in all the flour until you have a soft pliable dough. Knead the dough for a few minutes then leave in a clean, lightly oiled mixing bowl covered with a damp tea towel in a warm place for 4–6 hours, until risen and doubled in size.

2 When the dough has risen, knock down and knead again for a further 2–3 minutes. Take a portion of dough, about the size of a tennis ball, roll into a ball, then flatten between your hands into an oval disc. Roll out on the work surface to approximately 5cm (2in) thickness. Repeat this procedure until all the dough is used.

3 To cook the Naan, heat a large heavy-based frying pan (cast iron is best) or griddle until it is very hot; this may take up to 5 minutes. Place the first Naan in the pan and cook on each side for 30 seconds. Repeat with the remaining Naan, keeping them warm on a plate, covered with a tea towel or aluminium foil. The Naan may be prepared in advance to this point.

4 When ready to serve, toast them lightly on both sides under a pre-heated grill until golden brown on each side. Spread with a little butter or ghee and serve hot.

Lamb Biryani

Serves 4–6

900g (2lb) leg of lamb, boned,
    trimmed and cut into 2.5cm
    (1in) pieces
1–2 tablespoons vegetable oil
5 medium onions, peeled and thinly
    sliced (1 reserved for the rice)

for the spices

6 cloves garlic, crushed, peeled and
    finely chopped
1cm (1/2in) piece root ginger, peeled
    and finely chopped or puréed
1 green chilli, slit lengthways,
    deseeded and finely chopped
2 teaspoons red chilli powder
1/2 teaspoon turmeric powder
1/2 teaspoon salt, to taste
2 tomatoes, peeled and quartered
900ml (1 1/2 pints) water,
    approximately

for the rice

900g (2lb) basmati rice
1/2 teaspoon cumin seed
1/2 teaspoon salt, to taste
a little vegetable oil for frying
the reserved onion, peeled and
    thinly sliced

to finish

1/2 teaspoon egg yellow colouring
    powder, mixed with a little water
2 teaspoons garam masala powder
1cm (1/2in) stick cinnamon, crushed
1 teaspoon cumin seed
2 black cardamom, pods removed
2 bay leaves, crumbled and crushed
1/2 teaspoon freshly ground black
    pepper

Shahjahann used the recipe below to show me how to make a proper biryani. Until then, I had assumed like most people that the restaurant variety with rice, meat and vegetables mixed up was close authentic. Shahjahann's version is a colourful, layered work of art and it's much, much tastier.

1 First wash the prepared pieces of lamb, pat dry with kitchen paper and set aside. Put the rice into a roomy sieve and rinse it thoroughly under running water. Tip the rice into a large basin, cover generously with warm water and leave it to soak for 20–30 minutes. Then drain the rice back into the sieve and leave it to stand. Assemble all the remaining ingredients.

2 In a large heavy-based pan on a moderate flame heat up the oil and fry four of the sliced onions until they are golden brown. Then add the ginger, garlic and green chilli and stir-fry for 1 minute.

3 Now add the chilli powder, turmeric powder, salt to taste and tomatoes and stir-fry gently for a further minute.

4 Add the lamb and stir-fry for about 5 minutes as the meat begins to seal and take on some colour.

5 Now stir in the water and bring to a gentle simmer. Cover the pan and cook on a low to moderate flame for between 45 minutes and 1 hour or until the lamb is tender and the sauce has reduced somewhat.

6 Meanwhile, to cook the rice, bring a large pan three-quarters filled with water to the boil and add the 1/2 teaspoon cumin seed and salt. When the water is boiling add the rice and simmer until the rice is nearly done – about 8 minutes. The grains should still be hard in the centre. Drain and set aside.

7 Heat up a little oil in a small frying pan and fry the remaining thinly sliced onion until golden brown. Set aside.

8 To assemble the Lamb Biryani, put one-third of the rice into the base of a large pan and smooth it over into an even layer. Sprinkle with one-third of the egg yellow colouring, one-third of the garam masala powder and the whole spices and one-third of the fried onions. Cover the rice with one-third of the lamb, then repeat the layering process until all the ingredients are used.

9 Cover the pan with a tight-fitting lid. (If necessary line the lid with a sheet of aluminium foil to make a proper seal.) Put the pan on a very low flame to steam-cook gently for about 15 minutes. Test the rice by pinching a few grains or prodding gently with a knife – the grains should be tender and separate.

10 Serve with Green Chutney (see page 66).

Gobi Gosht

Serves 4

900g (2lb) shoulder of lamb, trimmed, boned and cut into 4cm (1¹/2in) pieces
1¹/2 teaspoons salt
1 medium onion, peeled and chopped
4 cloves garlic, crushed, peeled and finely chopped
4 whole bay leaves
2 black cardamom, pod removed, seeds crushed
4cm (1¹/2in) piece root ginger, peeled and finely chopped or puréed
2 tablespoons vegetable oil
3 medium ripe tomatoes, peeled and quartered

for the spices
1¹/2 teaspoons coriander seed and 1¹/2 teaspoons cumin seed, mixed together
1–2 teaspoons red chilli powder
1 teaspoon asafoetida (hing) powder
1¹/2 teaspoons turmeric powder
150ml (¹/4 pint) water
2 green chillies, slit lengthways, deseeded and flesh chopped
1 medium cauliflower, washed and trimmed into florets (or try potatoes or any other prepared vegetable)

to finish
handful fresh coriander leaves

to serve
1–2 teaspoons garam masala
sprinkling of fresh coriander leaves

If you're a beginner at these types of dish, I'd say you need to be a bit brave and spontaneous with adding the water – I've tried my best to give reassurance in the instructions. I recommend dry-roasting the cumin and coriander as this really does make a difference. Go easy on the red chilli the first time!

1 For the preparation before cooking, first wash the prepared pieces of lamb, pat dry with kitchen paper and set aside. Dry-roast the coriander and cumin seed in a heavy-based frying pan. Grind these spices in a blender or food processor, then prepare and assemble the remaining ingredients.

2 Heat a large heavy-based pan on a medium flame, then add the lamb, salt, onion, garlic, bay leaves, cardamom and ginger. Stir so the lamb takes on some colour and the onions begin to soften in the lamb's own fat and juices, then leave to cook gently until the lamb is tender, about 20–30 minutes.

3 Now add the vegetable oil and gently stir in the tomatoes. Cover and continue cooking for a minute or two, then add the ground coriander and cumin seed, red chilli, asafoetida and turmeric. Stir in a splash or two of water (4–6 tablespoons) to create the sauce. Lower heat and re-cover the pan; continue cooking for a further 10–15 minutes.

4 Add the green chillies and the cauliflower. Continue cooking, adding a little more water if necessary (not too much) and when the cauliflower is very nearly al dente stir in the fresh coriander and cook for a minute or two more. At this stage, if necessary, add a little more water and simmer to create more sauce and a fairly wet dish.

5 Spoon the finished dish into a warmed serving dish and sprinkle with 1–2 teaspoons of garam masala and a few fresh coriander leaves.

Chapati

Makes 12–14

*450g (1lb) chapati flour, or
wholewheat flour
good pinch salt (optional)
450ml (¾ pint) water,
approximately*

1 Sieve the flour and salt into a mixing bowl. Add the water gradually, drawing in all the flour to form a pliable dough. Knead on a lightly floured board for about 10 minutes, or use a mixer with a dough hook. Cover and leave to rest for ½–1 hour.

2 Divide the dough into 12 equal-sized pieces, rolling each into a ball. Lightly flour your hand, flatten each dough ball between your hands, place on a lightly floured surface and roll out to about 12.5–13cm (5–5½in) diameter. Do not to work in too much excess flour when rolling the dough because this may cause the texture of the cooked Chapatis to become dry. Keep the rolled-out Chapatis covered with a damp towel.

3 Heat up a large heavy-based frying pan or griddle until it is very hot; this may take up to 5 minutes. Place the first Chapati in the pan and cook on each side until bubbles of brown spots appear. Repeat with the remaining Chapatis, keeping them warm on a plate, covered with a tea towel or aluminium foil.

4 You can finish them by using tongs to hold each Chapati over the gas flame on a separate burner for a few seconds on each side, for further colouring and to make the Chapatis puffed up, light and fluffy.

Mango Lassi

*2 large ripe Indian mangoes
400g (14oz) natural set yoghurt
ice cubes
sugar to taste*

I know it is not always easy in Britain to get fresh mangoes but whenever possible, try to use fresh ones for this sumptuous drink, but you can substitute drained, tinned mango fruit. I have made it with chilled soya milk and chilled fresh mangos and I must say, it is to die for on a hot summer's day. It could even be all the meal you'd want at regular intervals on a very hot day!

1 To peel and cube the mangoes, take a thick slice from each side of the fruit, cutting as close to the stone as possible. Now peel the skin and flesh around the stone with a small vegetable knife and cut the flesh into cubes. Spoon out and cube the flesh from the two thick slices.

2 Put the mango, yoghurt and a few ice cubes in the bowl of a blender or liquidiser and blend until the lassi is smooth and of a drinking consistency. Add sugar to taste and a little crushed ice when serving in tall chilled glasses.

Chapter 5: Irish

'Romantic Ireland's dead and gone', wrote W.B. Yeats, but I'm not so sure about that. It still looks pretty romantic to me. The landscape hasn't been built on and modernised as much as most places in Europe. And in sympathy with their lovely surroundings, the people have managed to keep a poetic frame of mind, so they have! A lot of imagination and memory. I like places with a few spirits floating around, and Ireland is full of them.

Quite a lot of the Irish myths and legends relate to food in one way or another. Babies are found in the cabbage patch. A blindfolded virgin pulls up a cabbage and then inspects its root to get an idea of what her future husband will be like. The girl who gets the ring in her slice of barmbrack at Hallowe'en will be the next to marry. In pre-history, the Dagda, a great Celtic god, used to eat from a giant cauldron in which whole sheep and goats were boiled up with vast quantities of porridge and a hundred gallons of milk. The young hero Fionn Mac Cumhaill became the wisest of men by eating the salmon of knowledge. And of course the old Irish epics are full of cattle raids.

Actually the cattle raid is not the only point at which food and illegality come together. Many a poor family's diet has been supplemented by salmon poached from the private river of the big estate. In Seamus Heaney's poem 'A Constable Calls', a farmer is trying to avoid tax by concealing just 'a line of turnips'. After Guinness and whiskey, Ireland's most noteworthy drink is the poteen from illicit stills which manage to operate in remote spots in spite of the best endeavours of the Customs officers.

This (rather healthy) disrespect for the law must be something to do with hundreds of years of British rule. The Anglo-Normans came first in the twelfth century. The people have had to stand by and watch while the edible riches of their country was eaten by the landlords or shipped abroad. That's one reason that it's hard to define a national Irish cuisine: the rulers looked to England for their culture. And that's also partly to blame for the terrible catastrophe of the Famine: when the potato crops failed, there was other good food around but the poor couldn't get their hands on it.

Of course the spud does occupy a special place in the cooking. The Irish are connoisseurs of it. Colcannon is a simple but luscious mix of cabbage and potato. Boxty is mash plus raw grated potato, combined with flour and fried. Dispute whether or not to add carrots to the classic Irish stew, but there's no way you can omit the potato! And when they're sweet and delicate, as some varieties can be, I'm happy to be Irish and enjoy boiled spuds all by themselves – oh, well, with a little salt, butter and parsley, then.

The trouble is that I'm starting to feel guilty about perpetuating a very, very misleading stereotype: that Irish food begins and ends with potatoes. In fact such a clean, green, rain-swept country is bound to produce fine things to eat, and it does. The cattle have the smell of wild garlic on their breath, and the sheep are plump and happy on their lush pastures. Venison has been a staple here for thousands of years – archaeologists have found prehistoric roasting pits. It's a great place for game and wildfowl: not only your regular pheasant and pigeon, but rarer things like woodcock, snipe and barnacle geese.

The waters around this little island, stuck out as it is into the clean currents of the Atlantic, teem with edible wildlife. Here are herring, mackerel, bream, sole and cod, which used to be sold as salt fish like in the Caribbean. And there's crab, Dublin Bay prawns, lobster, crawfish, cockles, mussels – and oysters in profusion. These days, sadly, price is part of their image: someone quipped 'Don't eat oysters unless there's a pay-check in the month.' But a hundred years go in Ireland you could buy a turf-basket containing six hundred for sixpence!

These days, too, happily, the Irish are using all their wonderful natural resources to the full. There are famous cookery schools. New cheeses are being made. Sure, you can get pigs' feet and cabbage: but you can also go on an unforgettable gastronomic tour. No wonder Irish people around the world keep going home!

Smoked Haddock & Mussel Soup

Serves 4–6

for the mussels
2.3kg (5lb) fresh mussels (weight in their shells)
2 spring onions, trimmed and finely chopped, including the green parts
bunch fresh mixed herbs (thyme, parsley, sage and chives), chopped
2 glasses (300ml/½ pint) dry white wine

for the soup
50g (2oz) butter
1 large onion, peeled and very finely chopped
225g (8oz) fillets of naturally smoked haddock
600ml (1 pint) reserved mussel liquor (if necessary make up quantity with water or dry white wine)
450–700g (1–1½lb) Kerr's Pinks or Golden Wonder potatoes, cooked and mashed with a little milk
600ml (1 pint) full cream milk or 450ml (¾ pint) milk, mixed with 150ml (¼ pint) double cream
freshly ground black pepper, to taste

to finish
generous handful of chopped parsley

Ireland's extensive coastline has always thrown up a prodigious quantity of excellent fish, and in particular shellfish – much of which was gathered by the worn and weary hands of the women and their young children. Hauled by the wicker basket-load, most was sold on for ready cash, while more reached the open hearth, especially on fast and holy days and during the forty days of Lent.

1 Wash and scrub the mussels under running cold water, scraping off any barnacles and pulling off the hairy threads. The shells should be tightly closed. If any shells are gaping open and do not clamp shut when tapped, discard them. Mussels with cracked shells should also be discarded.

2 To steam open the mussels, first put the spring onions, herbs and wine into a large pan or stock pot on a high flame and bring up to the boil. Add the mussels and steam until the shells open, using a perforated spoon to remove them as they open and transfer them to a colander set over a bowl to catch their liquor. Steaming open the shells takes about 5 minutes; do not overcook the mussels or they will become tough. Discard any that fail to open. Depending on the size of the pan, steaming the mussels may have to be done in two or three batches. Strain and reserve the liquor for the soup. (If necessary, make up the quantity of liquor to 600ml (1 pint) with water or a little more dry white wine.) When cooled, pick out the mussels, set aside, and discard the shells.

3 Heat the butter in a large heavy-based pan on a moderate flame. When the butter foams, turn the flame to low, tip in the onion and cook until soft and transparent. Put the haddock, skin side down, into the pan, cover with the mussel liquor and simmer for about 5 minutes until the fish is barely at the point of flaking. Remove it to a plate and, when cooled somewhat, remove the skin and any stray bones. Flake and set aside.

4 Meanwhile add the cooked mashed potato to the pan and whisk to incorporate into the liquid. Add the milk, or milk and cream, bring up to a gentle simmer, add the flaked smoked haddock and continue cooking at a very gentle simmer for a further 5–10 minutes. Finally add the mussels to just heat through, check the seasoning and add pepper to taste (the smoked haddock will probably provide enough saltiness).

5 Ladle the soup into warmed bowls, sprinkle with chopped parsley and serve hot with a good Irish cheese and Brown Soda Bread (see page 92).

Potato & Smoked Bacon Soup

Serves 4–6

50g (2oz) butter
1 large onion, peeled and finely
    chopped
110g (4oz) streaky bacon, de-rinded
    and cut into large dice
450–550g (1–1¼lb) potato, peeled
    and cubed
900ml (1½ pints) ham bone or
    bacon stock
1½ teaspoons thyme, chopped
freshly ground black pepper, to taste

to finish
fresh single or double cream

Potatoes and bacon – the two stalwart ingredients of any Irish kitchen – pair up here to deliver a tasty and filling country style soup. Along with fine foodstuffs like Irish butter, cream and oatmeal, bacon and potatoes must stand out as classic Irish ingredients and to this day endure as popular traditional foods.

1 Heat the butter in a large heavy-based pan on a moderate flame. When the butter foams, tip in the onion and bacon and fry gently until the onion is soft and the bacon crisp.

2 Now add the cubed potatoes and stir them in the butter and bacon juices until glistening and golden. Turn the flame to low and continue cooking for about 5 minutes.

3 Stir in the stock, turn up the flame and bring to boiling point. Lower the flame and simmer gently until the potatoes are soft and tender. Check the seasoning and add freshly ground black pepper to taste (the bacon will probably provide enough saltiness).

4 Pour the soup into a blender or liquidiser and whizz until completely smooth. Serve hot in warmed soup bowls, each topped with a swirl of cream.

Dublin Coddle

Serves 4–6

450g (8oz) collar rashers or bacon
    pieces
1–2 onions, peeled and chopped
450g (8oz) butcher's good pork
    sausages
450g (8oz) potatoes, peeled and
    chunked, including some diced
    small to thicken the soup
handful of 'Soup Mix' (pearl barley,
    red lentils, split peas etc.)
water, or stock as available, to taste
freshly ground black pepper
salt, to taste

to finish
handful of chopped parsley

This soup or stew used to be a typical Saturday night dish in the Liberties area of central Dublin, especially relished after a night in the pub. In its day the Liberties was a very colourful and multifarious tenement area of Dublin. Recipes for the Coddle vary enormously and are as individual as Dubliners themselves! And a Dubliner living in Britain would not pass over a good Dublin Coddle for the sake of topography. However, the addition of potatoes remains highly controversial but as a personal choice, I prefer potatoes to crusty bread to mop up the juices.

1 Put all the ingredients into a large heavy-based pan on a moderate flame, bring to the boil, skim if necessary, turn the flame to low, cover the pan and simmer for about 1 hour, until all the ingredients are tender and cooked. (Do not add salt during the cooking – allow for the salt contained in the bacon and sausages.)

2 Taste and check the seasoning of the Coddle, adding salt if necessary. Spoon into warmed dishes, sprinkle with chopped parsley and serve with brown bread or Brown Soda Bread (see page 92).

Beef with Guinness

Serves 4–6

900g (2lb) stewing steak, skirt or chuck, cut into 5cm (2in) pieces
1–2 tablespoons vegetable oil or beef dripping
2–3 large onions, peeled and sliced
1 clove garlic, crushed, peeled and finely chopped
1 tablespoon plain flour
300ml (½ pint) Guinness
a little water, if needed
bouquet garni, or small bunch of fresh parsley, bay leaf and thyme
salt, freshly ground black pepper, pinch nutmeg, pinch sugar
1 teaspoon wine vinegar

I guess Guinness is as quintessentially Irish as you can get so inevitably, it has to crop up somewhere in Irish cuisine wherever the cooking takes place! This is succulence on a plate. It needs to be thick and creamy. This recipe was given to me by Sinéad ní Shuinéar and her daughter Julia who wrote me a great letter to tell me how much she enjoys my tv shows and accompanied by a drawing of her and me holding hands. This is for you Julia! Thanks.

1 Wash the trimmed, prepared beef, pat dry with kitchen paper and set aside.

2 Heat the oil or dripping in a large flameproof casserole on a moderate flame. Fry the meat in batches, turning them in the sizzling pan until browned all over. Do not overcrowd the pan. Use a perforated spoon to transfer each batch on to crumpled kitchen paper to drain.

3 Adding more oil or dripping if necessary, turn the flame down slightly and gently fry the sliced onions and garlic until soft and transparent. Sprinkle in the flour, stir well so that flour is cooked whilst absorbing all the oil or dripping.

4 Preheat the oven to 180°C/350°F/gas mark 4.

5 Return the meat to the casserole, pour in the Guinness and stir until the gravy becomes smooth and the casserole is gently simmering. If necessary add a little water to make up the liquid. Now add the herbs and seasonings. Cover the pan with a tight-fitting lid. If necessary line the lid with a sheet of aluminium foil to make a proper seal. Cook in the oven for about 1½–2 hours or until the meat is tender. Check and adjust seasoning if necessary.

6 Serve on warmed plates with the Winter Vegetables (page 90) and creamy mashed potato.

Irish Stew

Serves 4

900g (2lb) mutton or lamb chops
    (neck or shoulder for best results)
3–4 medium onions, peeled and
    roughly chopped
900g (2lb) potatoes, peeled and cut
    into 1cm (½in) rounds
4 carrots, peeled and chunked
    (optional)
salt and freshly ground black pepper
handful of parsley, chopped
1 generous sprig thyme
600ml (1 pint) water or mutton or
    lamb stock

to finish
handful of chopped curly parsley

Everybody has something to say about Irish stew. The argument about whether or not carrots should be included in this dish will I believe rage till time's end. What I say is that Irish stew is one of the tastiest and simplest stews you can get and when it's well made, it is second to none. It is worth cooking this very slowly for maximum effect.

1 Trim the meat of excess fat, cut each chop in half, rinse under running water and pat dry with kitchen paper.

2 Preheat the oven to 190°C/375°F/gas mark 5.

3 Put a layer of mutton or lamb in the base of a large heavy-based casserole. Cover with a layer of onion, potato and carrots (if using). Season generously with salt and freshly ground black pepper and sprinkle with some of the chopped parsley. Continue building up the layers of meat and vegetables until all the ingredients are used.

4 Pour in enough water or stock to just about the top of the stew; not quite covering. Push in the sprig of thyme.

5 Put the casserole on to a moderate flame and gently bring to the boil. Cover the pan with a tight-fitting lid and transfer to the oven to simmer gently for about 2 hours. Alternatively the stew can be gently simmered on a low flame on the hob.

6 Ladle the stew into warmed soup bowls, sprinkle with the chopped parsley and serve straight away.

Colcannon

Serves 6–8

1.15–1.4kg (2¹/₂–3lb) potatoes (Kerr's Pinks or Golden Wonder), unpeeled

salt

1 cabbage, spring or Savoy, quartered, outer leaves and core removed, leaves finely shredded across the grain

ham or bacon stock to cook the cabbage (optional), or water

freshly ground black pepper

4–5 large spring onions, trimmed and finely chopped, including the green parts

175ml (6fl oz) double or whipping cream

225g (8oz) butter

You might elect to peel the potatoes before boiling, but boiling them unpeeled really does result in a superior flavour.

1 Wash and scrub the potatoes but do not peel them. Put them in a pan of cold salted water on a moderate to high flame and bring to the boil. Cook at a steady gentle boil until the potatoes are tender, drain and leave to cool a little.

2 Meanwhile cook the cabbage in 1cm (½in) bacon stock or water. If using water, add salt. Cook briskly, adding a little more water or stock if necessary, for at least 10 minutes as the cabbage needs to be very soft and tender for the Colcannon. Drain, return to the warm pan, season with pepper, add a knob of butter, cover the pan and keep warm.

*3 Melt a scrap or two of butter in a small pan and fry the spring onions gently until soft; set aside and keep warm. Put the cream into another pan, bring up to just under simmering point, set aside and keep warm. Melt approximately 225g (8oz) butter in another small pan, set aside and keep warm.

*4 Now peel the potatoes, return them to the warm pan on a very low flame, season with a little salt and freshly ground black pepper and mash them thoroughly. Pour in the warm cream and beat until fluffy, then stir in the cabbage and spring onions and beat again – in general the potato and cabbage should be roughly in equal proportions.

5 Serve in individual warmed bowls. Make an impression on the top of each serving of Colcannon and pour a little lake of melted butter into each. Serve straight away.

*NOTE

This recipe uses a lot of pans so in an attempt to save a pan or two and flavour the cream at the same time, here's an alternative suggestion for steps 3 and 4:

3 Put the cream into a small pan on a low flame, add the spring onions and simmer gently for about 4–5 minutes until the onion is tender and the cream is flavoured. Set aside and keep warm. Melt the butter in a small pan; set aside and keep warm.

4 Now peel the potatoes, return them to the warm pan on a very low flame, season with a little salt and freshly ground black pepper and mash thoroughly. Pour in the warm cream and spring onions and beat until fluffy, then stir in the cabbage and beat again – in general the potato and cabbage should be roughly in equal proportions.

Winter Vegetables

Serves 4 as an accompaniment

Peel and chunk equal quantities totalling about 900g (2lb) swede and parsnip. Peel about 450g (1lb) carrots and dice them quite small. Put them all into a large pan, cover with cold water, add a pinch of salt, bring to the boil, turn down the flame, and simmer until the vegetables are cooked – about 20 minutes. Drain, reserve the cooking water, return the vegetables to the warm pan, add plenty of butter, salt and freshly ground pepper to taste and mash to your preference, adding a little of the cooking liquid as necessary. Turn into a warmed serving dish, dot with scraps of butter and serve.

Potato Cakes

450g (1lb) potatoes (Kerr's Pinks or
Golden Wonder), unpeeled
1 teaspoon salt
25–50g (1–2oz) butter, melted
110g (4oz) plain flour
pinch of freshly ground black pepper
a little butter or bacon fat for frying
(optional)

Great with bacon or spread with butter and sprinkled with a little sugar. Older potatoes are best for this recipe because they are floury.

1 Wash and scrub the potatoes but do not peel them. If using old potatoes, put them in a pan of cold salted water on a moderate to high flame and bring to the boil. Young potatoes should be added to boiling salted water. Cook at a steady gentle boil until the potatoes are tender.

2 Drain the potatoes; peel as soon as you can handle them, bearing in mind that the best potato cakes are made whilst the potatoes are still hot.

3 Mash the potatoes to a smooth, lump-free consistency, add a pinch or two of salt and freshly ground black pepper and pour in the melted butter.

4 Put the mashed potatoes into a mixing bowl and gradually incorporate enough flour to knead the mixture into a soft, pliable and manageable dough. Do this quickly and lightly and do not overhandle the dough or the potato cakes will be heavy.

5 Heat up a griddle or large cast-iron frying pan on the stove top, but do not add any butter or fat.

6 Roll out the dough on a lightly floured working surface to form a 0.5–1cm (¼–½in) thick round. Cut the round into triangles – farls – or use a cutter to make small individual round potato cakes.

7 Cook the potato cakes on the hot griddle or frying pan, turning once or twice, until both sides are mottled and golden brown. Alternatively the cakes can be fried in a little butter or bacon fat.

Irish Apple Cake

Serves 10–12

for the apple filling
900g (2lb), approximately 5–6
    medium to large cooking apples,
    eg Bramley Seedlings, peeled,
    cored and sliced
100ml (4fl oz) water, approximately
2 tablespoons sugar
generous pinch of cinnamon

for the cake
225g (8oz) butter, cubed
225g (8oz) caster sugar
275g (10oz) self-raising flour
3 large eggs, free-range if possible,
    beaten
a little milk to mix
scrap of butter for greasing
granulated sugar for sprinkling

to finish
whipped cream or home-made
    custard

In Ireland any festive or celebratory occasion is incomplete without the presence of an apple cake or tart and apples really are the lords and ladies of traditional Irish dessert dishes, turning up in anything from cakes to crumbles and fools to puddings. A great favourite was, and still is, Irish Apple Cake which can be made in a variety of ways. In its simplest guise apples were layered through a sweetened soda bread dough and baked over the open fire in a cast iron enclosed 'bastible' pot. Some people like to enrich the dough by using eggs and milk in the place of buttermilk, while others favour mixing the apples through the dough rather than layering them in the traditional fashion. In this recipe below, Regina Sexton, who gave it to me, says she chose this lighter version because her mum makes it that way and it also allows the apples to be cooked a little before layering through the mixture.

1 To make the filling, put the prepared apples into a medium heavy-based pan on a low to moderate flame, add the water and bring slowly to a gentle simmer. Cook the apples very gently for about 5–6 minutes, or until the fruit is slightly softened and still whole. Do not overcook, break up or reduce the apples to a mush. Add the sugar and cinnamon and stir gently until dissolved. Set aside and leave to cool.

2 Meanwhile grease a small roasting tin – approximately 25 x 33cm (10 x 13in) and preheat the oven to 190°C/375°F/gas mark 5.

3 Put the butter and sugar into a mixing bowl and beat thoroughly to a light, fluffy, pale-coloured cream. Add in about one-third of the beaten egg and a tablespoon of flour at a time, beating well after each addition. Fold in the remaining flour, if necessary adding a little milk to give a dropping consistency.

4 Spread just under half the mixture into the base of the roasting tin and cover evenly with the apple filling. Top with the rest of the cake mixture, spreading it evenly. Sprinkle liberally with granulated sugar. Bake in the oven for 50–55 minutes, or until nicely browned and cooked through.

5 While still in the tin, cut the cake into squares and serve hot or cold with whipped cream or home-made custard.

Barmbrack

Start the day before for soaking the fruit

275g (10oz) currants
110g (4oz) sultanas
50g (2oz) raisins
225g (8oz) brown sugar
300ml (½ pint) cold strong tea approximately (no milk or sugar added!)
450g (1lb) plain flour
1 teaspoon baking powder
2 eggs

A very traditional bread or 'sweet cake', dense with fruit and wonderful for breakfast. Intimately associated with the Celtic festival of Hallowe'en. As part of the fortune telling associated with that holiday, various things are baked into it, most basically a ring (for marriage) and a (well washed, paper-wrapped) penny (for wealth). Bewley's, Dublin's long-established coffee house cum bakery, does a yeasted variant, containing a ring only. The walls of one of its branches display framed copies of letters from visitors who, having bought a brack and taken it home, discovered to their horror that it contained what they took to be an employee's wedding ring, which they swiftly returned.

1 Put the dried fruit and sugar into a mixing bowl, cover with cold tea and leave to soak overnight.

2 The next day, pre-set the oven to 190°C/375°F/gas mark 5. Add the flour, baking powder and eggs to the soaked fruits and mix well to combine. Pour this thick batter into a greased loaf tin and bake in the oven for about 1½ hours. If necessary cover the loaf with aluminium foil or greaseproof paper to prevent the top from scorching. Test by inserting skewer or metal knitting needle into the middle of the cake. If it emerges cleanly, the loaf is cooked. Cool on a wire rack. Serve sliced and spread with butter. Keeps well.

Brown Soda Bread

400g (14oz) wholewheat flour
50g (2oz) oatmeal
450g (1lb) plain flour
1 teaspoon bicarbonate of soda
1 good teaspoon salt
40g (1½oz) butter, chilled
600g (1 pint) buttermilk

Yeast never made it into the average Irish kitchen, possibly because the softer local wheat doesn't respond well to it, possibly because yeast has always been highly suspect (closely associated with the brewing of poitín – moonshine).

1 Preheat the oven to 190°C/375°F/gas mark 5.

2 Put all the dry ingredients into a mixing bowl and combine. Rub in the butter, then gradually add the buttermilk to make a soft, pliable dough. Knead lightly on a lightly floured working surface and form into a large round, about 5cm (2in) thick. Use a knife to mark with a deep cross and put on a lightly floured baking sheet. Bake in the oven for 30–40 minutes. To test if the bread is cooked, turn it upside down and tap with fingertips – it will sound hollow when the bread is done. Cool on a wire tray.

Irish Coffee Cake

Serves 8–10

for the cake
175g (6oz) self-raising flour
½ teaspoon baking powder
150g (5oz) caster sugar
110g (4oz) butter, diced, room
  temperature
2 large eggs, free range if possible,
  beaten
1 tablespoon instant coffee dissolved
  in 3 tablespoons milk

for the butter cream icing
175g (6oz) icing sugar
50g (2oz) butter
1 teaspoon instant coffee dissolved
  in 50ml (2fl oz) Irish whiskey

to moisten
2–3 teaspoons icing sugar
1 teaspoon instant coffee
50ml (2fl oz) Irish whiskey

to decorate
50g (2oz) hazelnuts, toasted and
  chopped
chocolate shavings

to finish
whipped cream

Irish coffee, as the story goes, was invented at Shannon airport just after the Second World War. This luxuriously warming drink was the creation of the chief bartender, Joe Sheridan, who, on observing a great many American passengers shiver their way through his bar, decided to serve up the winning combination of very strong black coffee flavoured with Irish whiskey and topped with lightly whipped cream. The recipe below is inspired by this heart-warming beverage.

1 Grease a round cake or baking tin and preheat the oven to 200°C/400°F/gas mark 6.

2 Sieve the flour and baking powder into a large mixing bowl and add the remaining cake ingredients. Beat together using a hand-held mixer or begin with a wooden spoon and finish beating with a balloon whisk until the mixture holds the impression of the beater or whisk. Alternatively a food mixer can be used. Pour the mixture into the prepared cake tin, smooth the surface with a spatula and bake in the preheated oven for 25 minutes or until the cake is cooked. To test, insert a skewer or metal knitting needle into the middle of the cake: if it emerges cleanly the cake is cooked. Leave in the tin for a few minutes, then turn out onto a wire rack and cool.

3 Meanwhile make the coffee butter cream icing. Sieve the icing sugar into a mixing bowl, add the remaining ingredients, beat well to incorporate then cream until soft. Set aside.

4 For moistening the cake, dissolve the sugar and coffee in the whiskey and set aside.

5 Slice the cooled cake in half horizontally. Turn the top half over and moisten both of the cut halves with the flavoured whiskey, letting the mixture seep well in. Now use half of the coffee butter cream icing to sandwich the cake back together.

6 Spread the remaining icing mixture over the top of the cake, smooth with a palette knife and decorate with the nuts and chocolate shavings.

7 To serve, slice into thin wedges and, to complete the Irish Coffee allusion, serve with plenty of whipped cream.

Caragheen Moss Blancmange

Serves 4–6

for the blancmange
7–10g (¼–½oz) dried carragheen moss
900ml (1½ pints) full fat milk
a few slivers of lemon rind
2–3 drops vanilla essence, or vanilla pod
1 large egg, free range
2–3 tablespoons sugar

for the whiskey cream
150ml (5fl oz) double or whipping cream
2–3 teaspoons icing sugar (optional)
2–3 tablespoons Irish whiskey

Be careful with quantities of moss used. If too much is added, the pudding will have a pronounced taste of the sea. Carragheen blancmange has a decidedly delicate flavour that can be relished on its own or enlivened with the fruity zest of stewed gooseberries or blackberry compôte. Alternatively, simply serve with a dribble of honey and the whiskey cream given in this recipe.

1 Soak the carragheen in warm water for 10–15 minutes. This rejuvenates the moss and releases any trapped sand or tiny pebbles.

2 Drain and discard the water and put the moss, milk, lemon rind and vanilla essence or pod if using into a pan on a moderate flame. Bring to the boil, then simmer gently for 20–25 minutes. As the mixture gently cooks it will slowly and visibly begin to thicken and swell.

3 Meanwhile separate the egg and beat the yolk and sugar in a roomy mixing bowl until pale in colour. Reserve the egg white.

4 Strain the carragheen and milk mixture into a jug, which will slightly cool it, then pour onto the sugar and egg yolk, beating and drawing together the mixture. Set aside to cool and settle.

5 Whisk the egg white until stiff then fold in to the carragheen mixture and put the bowl in the refrigerator to set. If the pudding is to be moulded, use a wetted mould to ensure easy release of the pudding.

6 To make the whiskey cream, lightly whip the cream and icing sugar (if using) and stir in the whiskey. If the cream sinks a little after the whiskey is added, whip again lightly for a few seconds.

Chapter 6: Scottish

When you walk through the hills and by the lochs of Scotland, the sheer beauty of the place – the colours of the mountains, the open skies, the untouched wilderness, the deafening stillness punctuated periodically by the crashing of the waves or the cries of wild birds – is just so aesthetic and absorbing that one can easily be lulled onto another plane, forgetting everything. I found myself staring open-mouthed at the loveliness of Loch Erribol and the surrounding paradise of birds circling overhead, the plump, white, fluffy sheep with black faces grazing on the hillsides and the signs of fish rising on the shiny, symphonic water. It was especially emotional for me because all my life I'd planned a visit to the homeland of one James Bannerman, my great-great-grandfather, who left for West Africa in the middle of the last century. Scotland didn't disappoint me.

Oysters and champagne – life doesn't get better in Scotland.

Ancestors aside, the Scottish countryside is brimming with fresh, natural foods and

those, I can assure you, were not wasted on me! Venison, pheasant, partridge, grouse, salmon, herring, scallops and oysters are all readily available; and should you get tired of them, there is always the haggis, porridge, oatmeal cakes, scotch broth and fresh cheeses to be washed down with a 'wee dram' of single malt whisky! But despite the natural larder that nature has bestowed upon this lucky country, the modern Scottish diet has come under regular criticism – too many chips, too much animal fat and sugar. It's a shame, because in reality that has nothing at all to do with the country's traditional cooking. In fact, I feel that the classic Scottish diet is one of the healthiest in the world. Whatever Dr Johnson said about oats as horse-fodder, they are just as beneficial to humans! Swiss muesli as a health-food is a great marketing success story, but the Scots have had oatmeal brose at the core of their diet for hundreds if not thousands of years.

Deer, grouse, hare and fish are not simply free-range – they are wild. The sheep and cattle too are particularly wholesome, grazing as they do on heather and mountain grasses. Within the living memory of older people I spoke to, bere-meal (hardy Scots barley), herrings and oysters were so much a staple that the poor were ashamed of them; and yet, in modern eyes that would rank as one of the world's most health-giving diets. Even haggis when made well, is quite a decent balance of offal and oatmeal. I suppose it's no good pretending that whisky is good for you as well – but the word in Gaelic means 'water of life', and it certainly tastes sort of, well, beneficial!

It may be a bit chilly and wet at times, but Scotland is actually a perfect environment for many great ingredients. Surprisingly, soft fruits like raspberry and rowanberry benefit from the long hours of summer light and the cool weather which keeps pests down. The change in eating habits has been, as everywhere, to do with lifestyles. Cooks need to be hanging around for long hours to keep an eye on the old 'girdle' and stock-pot. These were the twin pillars of the old Scottish kitchen, the former for scones and bannocks, the latter for 'broth'.

Of course long stewing is a classic way to deal with inexpensive food like the aging broiler chicken or tough cuts of mutton. But Scottish cooking is not all simple crofters' stuff. Far from it. The Auld Alliance with France was born over seven hundred years ago. Mary Queen of Scots was Queen of France for a while, too: and she brought back chefs who had their own ideas about *pot au feu*. Nothing could be more sophisticated than grouse stuffed with local cranberries and rowanberries; or more delicate than salmon marinated in spicy brine with juniper berries and molasses, then cold-smoked over oak wood from old whisky casks!

A Scotch Broth Dinner

Allow pre-soaking time for the pulses, if necessary

Serves 8

*1.4–1.8kg (3–4lb) scrag end of lamb
  or mutton*
*175g (6oz) pearl barley, pre-soaked
  if necessary*
*110g (4oz) dried split peas, pre-
  soaked if necessary*
4.8 litres (8 pints) water
*450g (1lb) carrots, peeled and diced
  small*
*450g (1lb) white turnip or swede,
  peeled and chunked*
225g (8oz) leeks, washed and sliced
*3 medium onions, peeled and
  chopped*
freshly ground black pepper
salt, to taste

to serve

*2–3 handfuls fresh parsley, finely
  chopped*
1.4kg (3lb) potatoes
*a little butter, milk and seasoning
  for mashing potatoes*

To dish up in the authentic Scottish, and particularly Caithness, way, serve the Scotch Broth Dinner in two courses, broth with Bere Scones, then the meat and vegetables.

1 Rinse the lamb or mutton under running water and put into a very large pan with the pearl barley and split peas (pre-soaked if necessary), cover with the water and bring to the boil on a moderate flame. Skim the froth from the surface of the broth, turn the heat to low and simmer gently for 30 minutes, skimming from time to time if necessary, until the broth is clear.

2 Now add all the prepared vegetables and a generous few turns of pepper. Cover the pan and continue to simmer very gently for 1–1½ hours or until the lamb is tender, adding salt to taste towards the end of the cooking time.

3 Meanwhile, peel and boil the potatoes in the usual way, draining when cooked and adding a little butter, warmed milk and seasoning and mashing to your preference. Spoon into a warmed serving dish, cover and keep warm.

4 To dish up, first warm shallow soup plates and scatter a handful of chopped parsley into each of them. Add large ladlefuls of the broth only and serve with Bere Scones.

5 Follow this first course by lifting the meat out of the pan with a perforated spoon and arranging on a large warmed serving platter. Surround the meat with the chunks of tender turnip and the remaining vegetables, spoon some of the broth all over the dish and scatter over some more chopped parsley. Take the platter to the table for serving, with the dish of mashed potatoes.

Peasemeal and Beremeal

Peasemeal is a yellow field pea grown in the Caithness area. It was also known in England as the protein pea. It does have a distinctive taste and there is no substitute for it in the Peasemeal recipes, according to Scottish cooks and Fergus Morrison at Golspie Mill in Sutherland, who is a member of the Traditional Cornmillers Guild and produces it at his mill. He supplies it to Green City Wholefoods in Glasgow, who are the main wholesalers and distributors (it's known as brosemeal in this city). Ryans Wholesalers of Edinburgh too, although they do not supply such a wide area. At present the only place in England where it may be possible to buy it is at Chatsworth Farm Shop, near Bakewell, Derbyshire.

Beremeal is also special to the Caithness area. It is an ancient and genetically pure barley and essential to the recipe for Bere Scones (Bannocks). Available from Green City Wholefoods and Ryans Wholesalers.

Cock-a-Leekie Soup

Start soaking the prunes a day ahead
of cooking

Serves 8
110g (4oz) prunes
1 medium chicken
2 rashers streaky bacon, de-rinded
  and diced
2 large leeks, cleaned and cut into
  rings
1.7 litres (3 pints) water
2 teaspoons salt
sprinkling of pepper

In some parts of Caithness 2 tablespoons of pinhead oatmeal are added for the last 30 minutes, turning this classic soup into a creamy oatmeal version.

1 Soak the prunes for 24 hours in cold water. Put the whole chicken, the bacon pieces and salt into a large heavy-based pan, cover with the water and bring slowly to the boil. Reserve about a quarter of the leeks and add the rest to the pan. Sprinkle with pepper, cover and simmer for 3 hours. Skim off any froth from the surface from time to time, until the broth is clear.

2 Carefully remove the chicken from the pan and cut the meat into large serving pieces, cover with aluminium foil and keep warm. Stone the prunes and add them to the soup along with the meat and remaining leeks. Taste and add more salt if necessary. Simmer for 30 minutes.

3 Put a slice or two of the warm chicken into each soup plate and ladle over the soup and the prunes, although some people prefer to remove the prunes before serving.

Tatties and Herring

salt herrings – 2 per person
tatties (potatoes) – Golden Wonders
  or some other tasty dry-fleshed
  variety – 4 medium-size potatoes
  per person
glasses of cold milk
finger bowls and spare napkins

Salt herrings were exported in wooden barrels during the last two centuries from Wick to every country in Europe as well as to the West Indies to feed the plantation slaves. It was the staple diet of the poor who were ashamed to admit to eating salt herring. Parents told their children to call the meal something bigger and more grand. One small boy shouted to his dad to come for dinner because the whales were ready.

1 Wash the salt herring and soak overnight in cold water. Scrub the potatoes but leave their skins on as they must be boiled in their jackets.

2 Put the potatoes on to boil in a large pan of salted water. In a second pan of water bring the herring to the boil and immediately change the water. Bring to the boil again and shut off the heat.

3 When the poatoes are cooked serve 2 herrings and 4 potatoes. Traditionally the meal

should be eaten with your fingers, thus the finger bowls and spare napkins. Use a knife and fork if you must but be careful with the bones. Eat both the soft and hard roes.

Drink plenty of milk and enjoy this present-day delicacy. Should you feel thirsty afterwards drink cold water.

Oyster Peasemeal Pâté

5 oysters
2 cloves garlic, crushed, peeled and
   roughly chopped
25g (1oz) butter
40g (1½oz) peasemeal
   (see ingredients note)
½ teaspoon paprika or pounded
   mace
15g (½oz) coarse oatmeal or
   sesame seed
4 tablespoons double or
   single cream
1–2 teaspoons lemon juice, to taste
freshly ground black pepper
   (optional)

1 Open the oysters (see panel on page 102 for instructions on opening). Take care to keep the oyster liquor in the shell.

2 Put the oysters, their liquor and the garlic into a blender or liquidiser and whizz to a purée.

3 Melt the butter in a small heavy-based pan on a low to moderate flame, add the peasemeal, paprika and oatmeal, and stir to mix. Add the oysters and chopped garlic, stirring continuously until just simmering. Now add the cream and lemon juice and continue to stir the mixture at just under simmering point for 3–4 minutes. The amount of moisture the peasemeal absorbs varies so, after cooling, it may be necessary to add a little more cream to obtain the preferred consistency. Taste and adjust the seasoning, add a squeeze more lemon and freshly ground black pepper if using. Chill and serve in individual ramekins.

Variation:
Add 40–50g (1½–2oz) flaked fresh or smoked fish (fresh or smoked salmon, mackerel or haddock) at the final stage of cooking.

Oyster Sausages

serves 2

18 small plump oysters
275g (10oz) soft breadcrumbs
275g (10oz) shredded vegetable suet
pinch salt
pinch cayenne pepper
pinch pounded mace and grated
  nutmeg
2 eggs, beaten

to finish

seasoned dry breadcrumbs for
  coating
vegetable oil for frying

Angela MacKay is from Achnahuaigh (pronounced achnewhoargh), a very pretty village on the sea at the northwest end of Sutherland in Scotland. Angela is a diminutive, well-rounded, generous Scottish woman with a laughing voice which sounds like water tumbling out of a bottle. Angela is a vital mother earth and has shared many of her recipes with me.

1 Open the oysters: see panel for instructions.

2 Roughly mince the oysters. This can be done by chopping them very finely on a board or giving them one or two quick pulses in the bowl of a blender or liquidiser. Put them in a mixing bowl with their liquor.

3 Add the breadcrumbs, suet and seasonings to taste and stir thoroughly to combine. Gradually add the beaten eggs, stirring in enough to form a softish pliable paste – the consistency of sausage meat. Cover the bowl and leave in a cool place for two or three hours.

4 Now shape pieces of the mixture into sausages and roll them in the seasoned breadcrumbs to coat lightly. Heat up the vegetable oil in a heavy-based frying pan on a moderate flame and gently fry the sausages, turning them from time to time, until they are evenly golden brown.

5 Serve hot – try them with grilled bacon and mushrooms.

Opening oysters

Use a tea towel around one hand to help you get a grip on the oyster, making sure it lies flat side up in the palm of your protected hand. Insert the blade of the oyster knife, or a short stout kitchen knife, into the hinge of the oyster, about 1cm(½in) and prise it open. Slide in a small sharp knife to cut away the 'moorings' from the top and bottom halves of the shell. Pull off the top part of the shell, and with the tip of your knife flick out any flakes of shell that may have fallen on top of the oyster. Take care to keep the oyster liquor in the shell.

Angela's Oyster, Cream Cheese and Mushroom Pâté

To serve as an appetiser with toasts or crudités

6–8 large fresh Scottish oysters
1 glass sweet white wine (Angela uses a Mosel)
25g (1oz) butter
½ large onion, peeled and very finely chopped
225g (8oz) mushrooms, wiped and very finely chopped
250g (9oz) firm cream cheese
juice of ½ lemon (1–2 tablespoons)
good few turns of freshly ground black pepper, to taste

to finish
paper thin slices of halved lemon
sprinkling of finely chopped parsley

Paradoxically neither Angela nor I like raw oysters but she tells me that, until recently, oysters were always cooked. Eating oysters raw must be a modern fad. This, then, is one of many imaginative ways Angela finds to serve her oysters.

1 Open the oysters according to the instructions in the panel opposite.

2 Put the oysters and their liquor into a small pan with the white wine. Put the pan on a low flame, gently bring up to just under simmering and gently poach the oysters for about 2 minutes. Remove from the heat, drain off and reserve the poaching liquid (this can be frozen for future use in other dishes such as soups, chowders or sauces).

3 Melt the butter in a medium-sized heavy-based saucepan on a moderate flame and gently cook the chopped onions and mushrooms for 7–10 minutes until they are very soft and pale golden. Remove from the heat, drain and cool.

4 Now put the cream cheese into a blender or liquidiser, add the oysters, onions and mushrooms and switch on to purée. Add the lemon juice and black pepper and whizz to the consistency of a smooth pâté. Taste and check the seasoning and add more lemon juice or pepper if necessary.

5 Scoop out the pâté into a serving dish, smooth it over, garnish with the slices of lemon, sprinkle with a little parsley, chill and serve.

Pillows of Scottish Smoked Salmon with Crab

Serves 6

Begin preparation a minimum of 6 hours ahead or the day before

for the pillows of smoked salmon
350g (12oz) Scottish smoked salmon, thinly sliced
3–4 drops of olive or sunflower oil
175g (6oz) white crab meat, or pickled herring
1 avocado, stoned, peeled and cut into 0.5cm (1/4in) dice
50g (2oz) cucumber, peeled, sliced lengthways, deseeded, drained and cut into 0.5cm (1/4in) dice
1 large ripe plum tomato, peeled, deseeded and cut into dice
generous bunch of chives, finely snipped with scissors
juice of 1 lemon
sea salt and freshly ground black pepper, to taste

for the trout caviar cream
75g (3oz) trout caviar (if unobtainable use roe of salmon or lumpfish)
1 tablespoon horseradish sauce
150ml (1/4pint) double cream whisked to slightly thicken
150ml (1/4pint) crème fraîche
juice of 1 lemon
salt and white pepper

for the dressed cucumber
200g (7oz) cucumber
1–2 teaspoons Dijon mustard
75ml (3fl oz) balsamic vinegar
150ml (1/4pint) extra virgin olive oil
sea salt and ground black pepper
fresh herbs to taste, eg parsley, mint, chervil, finely chopped

to finish
a few sprigs of chervil or chives

1 Lightly oil six 10cm (4in) ramekins or moulds with a few drops of olive or sunflower oil. Measure and cut the sliced smoked salmon into strips approximately 20cm (8in) long. Use these strips to line the ramekins by draping the strips over and into each ramekin in a criss-cross fashion, leaving an overlap of approximately 2.5cm (1in) for folding over the filling.

2 Put all the ingredients for the pillows into a mixing bowl. If using pickled herring, rinse off the brine under running water, pat dry with kitchen paper, remove skin and flake the fish. Gently stir all the ingredients to combine, seasoning well with the lemon juice, sea salt and pepper. Taste to check seasoning.

3 Spoon the filling to two-thirds of the way up each of the lined ramekins, pressing down gently to mould with the back of a teaspoon. Fold the overlapping strips of salmon neatly over the filling, pressing down gently to seal, cover each ramekin with clingfilm and refrigerate for 6 hours or overnight.

4 To make the trout caviar cream, reserve 25g (1oz) of the caviar for garnish and mix together all the other ingredients in a small basin to a stiffish mousse-like consistency. Taste and check the seasoning, adding a squeeze or two more lemon juice or salt and white pepper if necessary.

5 Peel the cucumber (if wished), slice in two lengthways, scoop out seeds with a teaspoon and slice thinly into half-moon shapes. Put the mustard, balsamic vinegar, extra virgin olive oil and seasoning into a screw-top jar and shake to amalgamate. Taste and check the flavour: you may wish to add more vinegar or salt and pepper. Stir in a handful of finely chopped fresh herbs.

6 To serve the pillows of smoked salmon, remove the clingfilm from the first ramekin, run a knife round the edge to loosen the pillow, place a plate over the top, onto the centre of the plate. Repeat with the remaining ramekins.

7 Surround each pillow with an attractive arrangement of the sliced cucumber, with the balsamic vinegar dressing drizzled over. Put a spoonful of the trout caviar cream on top of each pillow, then garnish with the reserved caviar and a sprig of chervil. Serve with thinly sliced wholemeal bread.

Roast Venison with a difference

Serves 4–6

Begin preparation a day ahead for
marinating and making stock

900g–1.4kg (2–3lb) boned saddle or
leg of venison, bones reserved for
stock (allow 225g (8oz) boned
weight per serving)

for the marinade
3 juniper berries
sprig of thyme
sprig of rosemary
2 bay leaves
freshly ground black pepper
juice and zest of ½ orange
½ bottle of red wine
parsley stalks, roughly broken and
bruised

for the stock
venison bones, chopped
2 large onions, unpeeled, sliced in half
1 tablespoon olive oil, approximately
4 carrots, peeled and diced
2 leeks, cleaned, trimmed and
chopped
1 head of celery, cleaned, trimmed
and chopped
2 cloves garlic, crushed and peeled
2 teaspoons tomato purée
a few sprigs of thyme
6 peppercorns
3 bay leaves

for the garlic fondant potatoes
2–4 large baking potatoes, peeled
225g (8oz) clarified butter
1 whole head garlic
1–2 sprigs thyme

to finish
700g (1½lb) spinach leaves, de-ribbed
and washed
40g (1½oz) butter
sea salt and ground black pepper
watercress

1 Ask your butcher to trim the meat into serving portions, chopping and reserving the bones. Wash and pat dry with kitchen paper. Mix the marinade ingredients in a bowl, add the venison, turn to coat well, cover and leave in a cool place to marinate overnight.

2 To make the stock, first set the oven to 230°C/450°F/gas mark 8. Arrange the venison bones and unpeeled onion on the base of a roasting tin and roast in the oven for about 30–40 minutes. Do not add any oil. Turn the bones and onions occasionally. The bones and caramelised onion give a lovely colour and flavour to the stock.

3 Put the olive oil into a pan on a moderate flame, add the carrots, leeks, celery and garlic and fry gently until they are soft and golden brown, adding a little more olive oil if necessary. Add the tomato purée and continue cooking for a further minute. Pour in cold water to cover the vegetables, add the roasted bones and onions and scrapings from the roasting tin, the thyme, peppercorns and bay leaves and bring to the boil. Immediately turn down the heat to simmer, partially cover the pan and simmer for at least 3 or 4 hours, skimming occasionally. Drain into a bowl and set aside.

4 Pre-heat the oven to 230°C/450°F/gas mark 8. Slice the potatoes crossways into 1–2.5cm (½–1in) slices. Using an unfluted pastry cutter, cut and press out 3.5cm (1½in) rounds from the slices. Heat the clarified butter on a low flame. Slice the whole unpeeled head of garlic crossways in half. Put half, cut side down, into the simmering butter with the thyme, cook for a few minutes to flavour the butter. Add the potatoes and simmer for 20–30 minutes, turning once. Do not allow the butter to burn. When the potatoes are golden brown leave in the butter on a very low flame until ready to serve.

5 Melt a knob of butter in a pan, throw in the spinach and stir as it cooks briefly in the butter and the water clinging to the leaves. Cover, set aside and keep warm.

6 Heat up a little olive oil in a frying pan. Remove the venison (reserving the marinade), seal and sear it on both sides; immediately put them in the pan into the oven. This takes about 10 minutes usually. Transfer to a warm plate, 'tent' with foil, and keep warm.

7 Return the venison to the pan, add the marinade and deglaze by boiling fast. Add stock, bring up to simmering point and reduce to a flavoursome sauce, adding seasoning. Strain and keep warm. Slice the venison on the diagonal. Pour venison juice into the sauce. Put fondant potatoes in the centre of each plate, top with spinach, then sliced venison, and pour the thyme jus around. Garnish with watercress.

Roast Grouse with blackcurrants and marjoram

Serves 2

2 young grouse, cleaned
50g (2oz) butter, softened
75g (3oz) blackcurrants, rinsed and dried
2 tablespoons marjoram, chopped
salt and freshly ground black pepper
4 rashers streaky bacon
2 glasses red wine
1 heaped teaspoon blackcurrant or redcurrant jelly

Sue Lawrence, the *Sunday Times* cook and one of Scotland's greatest assets, makes this wonderfully rich and full-flavoured dish and she says that brambles and raspberries will also work. A wee dram will help to this entirely delicious dish!

1 Pre-heat the oven to 220°C, 425°F, gas mark 7. Clean the birds thoroughly by washing and drying them.

2 Mix together the softened butter, blackcurrants and marjoram, then season with salt and freshly ground black pepper. Carefully divide the stuffing between the grouse, spooning half into the cavity of each bird. Cover the breast of each grouse with two rashers of streaky bacon, then place them in a lightly oiled, heavy-based dish. Pour over the red wine.

3 Place in the oven for 15-20 minutes, depending on the size of your birds. Then, using a slotted spoon, remove the grouse to a carving board and cover with foil. Allow them to rest for at least 10 minutes before serving.

4 Place the roasting tin over a high flame and allow to bubble to reduce the liquid. Add the jelly and stir well to mix. Season to taste with salt and pepper and serve with seasonal vegetables.

Atholl Brose

Serves 2–4

110g (4oz) pinhead oatmeal
375ml (12fl oz) water (bottled
   Scottish spring water, if available)
250ml (8fl oz) good Scotch whisky
1–2 tablespoons heather honey, to
   taste, melted

Serves 2–4

2 tablespoons pinhead oatmeal
250ml (8fl oz) thick double cream
4 tablespoons good Scotch whisky
3 tablespoons heather honey, melted

As a drink: 1

1 Soak the pinhead oatmeal in the water for approximately one hour. Line a sieve with a piece of muslin and pour the mixture through this to drain into a jug, finally taking up the muslin and squeezing out the last drop of liquid.

2 Add the whisky to the liquid (the brose) and stir in the melted honey to taste. Pour the Atholl Brose into glasses and serve at room temperature, or chilled if preferred.

As a dessert

1 Put the pinhead oatmeal into a heavy-based frying pan and lightly toast under a moderate grill, or dry-fry on a moderate to low flame, giving the pan a shake from time to time, taking care not to scorch the oatmeal – about two to three minutes. Leave to cool.

2 Put the cream into a mixing bowl and whisk lightly to soft peak consistency; gently stir in the whisky and honey, and most of the toasted oatmeal, reserving some for garnish.

3 Spoon the Atholl Brose into serving dishes, sprinkle with some of the reserved oatmeal and serve.

As a drink: 2

'I never kent what rye was for/'til I had drunk the nectar'
Robert Louis Stevenson, in a poem in praise of Atholl Brose

I found that using local heather honey adds a new dimension both to the taste and identity of the brose.

To one cupful of oatmeal add an equal quantity of spring water. Mix to a creamy consistency in a glass bowl. Leave for half an hour, then squeeze and press the mixture through a sieve. The liquid that drains through forms the oatmeal 'brose'. Sweeten the brose with clear honey. The amount you use will vary according to your taste. A rough guide is eight teaspoons of honey – a little more can be added later when serving. Stir well and pour into an empty whisky bottle or decanter. Fill up with whisky, preferably a good Scottish malt. Shake well before serving, and sip slowly after a meal.

Crannachan

Serves 2–3

4 tablespoons pinhead oatmeal
250ml (8fl oz) double cream
4 tablespoons Drambuie
2 tablespoons heather honey
110g (4oz) fresh raspberries

1 Put the pinhead oatmeal into a heavy-based frying pan and lightly toast under a moderate grill, or dry-fry on a moderate to low flame, giving the pan a shake from time to time and taking care not to scorch the oatmeal. Leave to cool.

2 Put the cream into a mixing bowl and whisk lightly to soft peak consistency; gently stir in the Drambuie and honey to blend and fold in the fresh raspberries and most of the toasted oatmeal, reserving some for garnish.

3 Spoon the Crannachan into a serving dish and scatter over the reserved toasted oatmeal.

Scottish Shortbread

350g (12oz) plain flour
110 (4oz) caster sugar
110g (4oz) cornflour
pinch of salt
225g (8oz) salted butter
½ teaspoon vanilla essence
½ teaspoon lemon essence
a scrap of butter for greasing the
   baking trays

to finish
1 tablespoon caster sugar

1 Preheat the oven to 180°C/350°F/gas mark 4, and lightly butter one or two baking sheets.

2 Put the first four ingredients into a mixing bowl, mix together, then rub in the butter. Add the vanilla and lemon essence, then draw the mixture together and knead lightly and quickly into a dough. Roll the dough into a long sausage shape and slice into circles 0.5cm (¼in) thickness. Place these on the baking sheets and bake in the oven for about 15 minutes or until a pale gold colour and just firm to the touch.

3 Cool on a wire rack and sift over some caster sugar. Can be stored in an airtight tin.

Chapter 7: Jewish

The history of Jewish Britain started with the Norman invasion. They were expelled (without their possessions) two hundred years later, and it wasn't until they suffered a similar fate at the hands of the Spanish that they returned to these shores. They were joined in the East End of London by those escaping from Russia and Poland at the end of the 19th century. Then finally many came here to escape from the horrors of the thirties in Europe. But this thumbnail sketch doesn't touch on the amazing labyrinth of the lives and travels of these communities before they ended up in this country. I have friends who will talk for hours about Jewish history – if you let them!

The East End, incidentally, retains some Jewish features: Petticoat Lane Market, centre of the old rag trade, is big on Sunday but shut on Saturday. Cockneys still use the word 'kosher' to mean genuine, proper; they also picked up the Yiddish word 'nosh' and passed it on to the English language. But as they prospered, Jews moved up and out to North West London and to other parts of the country. Golder's Green has taken over as the focal point of Jewish Britain.

It's never good to be complacent, but in spite of all the hard knocks of their history, Jewish people in Britain today do not live in fear of persecution. The main worry for

Carmelli's bakery in Golders Green, London.

Café on the Green, where the bagels are brill.

them is that they will just slowly be diluted. Young Jews 'marry out', they give up the synagogue, they even stop eating chicken soup! As with all ethnic groups, assimilation to the local culture has an up and a down side. The very orthodox stick to arranged marriages, others just try to make sure their children meets the right type of partners. Rabbis make religion attractive with their jokes and wise stories. But I suspect that the most potent weapon in the armoury of Jewish parents and grandparents is their cooking. Not only is it distinctive and evocative, but they make it so good that no-one should want to opt out.

More than any other cuisine I know, every aspect of Jewish food, every dish and every ingredient seems to have a bit of history or religion or tradition attached to it. For starters there are those tricky kashrut (kosher) rules, of course, which not only exclude port, but also quite a lot of sea-food – in fact anything without scales and fins, so that's goodbye squid, eels, prawns, lobster and mussels. Then there's the difference between the Ashkenazi, who are from Russia and Northern Europe, and Jews from the rest of the world, who are known as Sephardi though the term orginally means 'Spanish'; most non-Askenazi have roots in the Mediterranean and Middle East, but did you know that there are also Indian and Chinese Jews? The British are better acquainted with Ashkenazi favourites like rollmop herrings, hot salt beef and bagels. But in line with the growing popularity of the Mediterranean diet, Sephardi food has been catching on in a big way. Look out for all those lovely Levantine ingredients like olives, chickpeas, dates, aubergine, lemon, mint and coriander.

Why is there so much chicken in the Jewish diet? Consult the history book again. The Jews in Central and Eastern Europe were not generally farmers, and they weren't rich: meat was expensive and had to be slaughtered in a kosher way, but they could raise the chickens themselves in the yard. Why the unleavened matzos – apart from the fact that in their bland way they're rather good? Consult the scriptures this time: when the Jewish people left Egypt in a hurry, they forgot to take their leaven. Hallah bread, cut ceremoniously at the start of the Friday night meal, symbolises the manna which the Israelites were given to eat in the wilderness.

On these pages and with these few words I can only skim the surface of a rich, deep and meaningful culture. I've offered (in cooking terms) only the 'appetisers' to explain Jewish food. To get the main course and the culture in all its complexities would require a tome of its own Whatever the stories behind them, there are lots of tasty and rather special Jewish dishes. And you don't have to be Jewish to make them. Why not try some of the luscious recipes on the next few pages, for a start!

Goldene Yoich (Chicken Soup)

Serves 6-8

1 large chicken, preferably a mature
  boiling fowl with giblets
cold water to cover
700g (1½lb) soup vegetables, to
  your preference, washed and cut
  into chunks
1 medium parsley root (petrushka)
  with leaves
bouquet garni, made with petrushka
  leaves, a few celery leaves, 2 bay
  leaves and a strip of lemon peel
a few peppercorns
salt to taste

I should think that hundreds of loving Jewish mothers could go to war over the exact ingredients for chicken soup! All sorts of vegetables can be included: onion leeks, carrots, celery leaves, parsnip, courgette and pumpkin – sometimes whole tomatoes for colour and flavour. One thing is for certain – try to find a proper boiling fowl (if possible with its feet still attached) and the giblets. Ad the parsley root (petrushka) is an essential flavour of the authentic soup. Restorative, efficacious, a miracle cure for colds? – yes, all of these, and soothingly delicious too.

1 Wash the chicken and giblets well in plenty of cold running water. If the feet are used, scorch them well over an open flame and rub to remove the hard skin.

2 Put the chicken, giblets and feet, if using, into a large heavy-based pan or stockpot, cover with cold water and bring very slowly to the boil on a moderate flame. Simmer for ten minutes, skimming from time to time to remove any froth.

3 Add the vegetables with the parsley root, bouquet garni and peppercorns and simmer very gently for three hours, skimming from time to time until the broth is clear.

4 If using a young roasting chicken, you may wish to use the chicken meat, chopped, for the soup. In this case, half way through the simmering time use two perforated spoons to remove the chicken from the broth. Strip the meat from the chicken and return the bones and carcass to the broth, reserving the tender meat for adding to the finished soup. In this way you will avoid having a chicken that is cooked to rags and of little further use in the dish.

5 At the end of the cooking time, taste and check the seasoning, adding a well judged pinch or two of salt to taste. Lift out the boiling fowl, if using, and strain the soup into another large pan. When it has cooled somewhat and the fat has risen to the surface, blot off with kitchen paper or skim – but leave a little fat to achieve the customary yellow globules which add sparkle to the soup.

6 Re-heat the soup and before serving add the reserved chopped chicken (if this was the method used), a handful of noodles (vermicelli), dumplings (Matzo balls, einlauf, nockerals or kneidlach) – or just simply a few pasta shapes.

7 Dish into warmed soup bowls, sprinkle with reserved chopped parsley leaves and serve.

Buboh

Serves 6

3 tablespoons vegetable oil
½ teaspoon turmeric
1cm (½in) root ginger, finely grated
2 fresh tomatoes, chopped
500g (1lb) chicken or fish (haddock
   or cod) cubed
2 fresh tomatoes, chopped
1 teaspoon salt
freshly ground black pepper to taste
3 cups rice, washed
1 chicken stock cube
1 tablespoon soya sauce
4 spring onions, finely sliced

This is an adaptation of the Chinese kai cheok, a soupy porridge, a sort of oriental chicken soup.

1 Heat oil, quickly stir in the turmeric and ginger. Add the tomatoes and toss for one minute, then add the chicken or fish, salt and pepper and mix until the meat is sealed.

2 Stir in the rice and cover with enough water to cook the rice. Crush and sprinkle the stock cube into the water. Stir to mix. Cover and bring to the boil on high heat. When it starts to boil, reduce the heat to moderate and simmer for about ½–¾ hour until the meat and rice are tender.

3 Serve hot with a drizzle of soya sauce, and garnish with the spring onions.

Egg and Aubergine Salad

Serves 4

1kg (2lb) aubergine, sliced
2 tablespoons vinegar
1 bay leaf
salt and freshly ground black pepper
2 hard boiled eggs
125g (5oz) onion, finely chopped
50-75g (2-3oz) mayonnaise
2 pickled cucumbers, finely chopped
capers for decoration

This dish is suggested for people who dislike the flavour of aubergine! It makes an interesting and easily prepared starter.

1 Cook the sliced aubergine in boiling salted water with a few drops of vinegar and a bay leaf for 20 minutes.

2 Drain and mince with the hard-boiled eggs and raw onion. Season with salt and freshly ground black pepper. Add the mayonnaise and cucumber and mix well. Decorate with capers.

Gehakle Leber

Serves 6

450g (1lb) chicken liver (or calf,
   goose or a mixture of poultry liver)
3 tablespoons Schmaltz (vegetarian)
110g (4oz) onion, chopped
salt and freshly ground black pepper
2 hard boiled eggs plus 1
for decoration (white and yolk
   separated and sieved)
parsley

1 Heat the schmaltz in a heavy-based frying pan over a medium flame. Fry the onion until nicely browned, then add the liver and fry until it is done to your liking. Season to taste with salt and pepper.

2 Either chop by hand, process or mince the liver and onion together with the hard boiled eggs. If the liver is too dry, moisten with some melted schmaltz.

3 Arrange on a flat platter and decorate with alternately coloured stripes made from the sieved yolks and whites of hard boiled egg. Border with parsley sprigs and serve chilled.

Hameem

Serves 6

1 whole chicken weighing around
   2kg (4lb)
2 medium onions, peeled and
   chopped
4 large, fresh tomatoes, peeled and
   chopped
1 teaspoon turmeric
1 cinnamon stick
3 cups long grain rice
4 tablespoons vegetable oil
salt and freshly ground black pepper
6 hard-boiled eggs, shelled

A dish traditionally served for the Sabbath lunch, after the synagogue service. The traditional method requires the removal of the skin of the chicken whole, it is then stuffed with all the other ingredients and cooked overnight over a damped charcoal fire with the cooking pot covered with heavy sacking. As this requires a tremendous amount of skill and time, this recipe that follows is the simpler one.

1 Heat three tablespoons of oil and fry the turmeric gently for thirty seconds then add the onions and sweat them for a few minutes. Add the tomatoes, salt, pepper and washed rice. Toss for two minutes.

2 Stuff the chicken cavity with three whole hard-boiled eggs and add some of the rice mixture. Place in a slow cooker and arrange the remaining rice and whole eggs around the chicken. Only cut the eggs in half when ready to serve.

3 Cover with half the water and the remaining 1 tablespoon of oil. Cook overnight on the lowest setting for around 12 hours; add more water in small amounts at a time as needed and keep warm until ready to serve.

Aloo Makala

Serves 6

1.5kg (3½lb) chicken, cut into 6
   portions
6 medium potatoes, peeled
6 medium carrots, peeled
6 medium onions, peeled and sliced
2.5cm (1in) root ginger, peeled and
   roughly chopped
1 teaspoon turmeric
1 stick cinnamon
4 cardamons
6 cloves
salt and freshly ground black pepper
10 tablespoons vegetable oil

1 Wash the chicken pieces and rub them with salt. Cut the potatoes and carrots in halves and then rub these and the onions with salt.

2 Heat the oil in a large saucepan. Fry the spices and ginger together for a minute. Add the chicken and keep tossing until the pieces are sealed. Cover the pan, turn down the heat and stir from time to time for about 15 minutes.

3 Drop in the potatoes, carrots and onions and mix well. Cover the pan again and cook on a low heat for about ½ hour, stirring occasionally, then remove the cover and cook until all the ingredients are well cooked and browned. Serve immediately.

Lamb Sania

Serves 4

700g (1½lb) lamb, finely minced
2 onions, peeled and finely sliced
4 tablespoons olive oil
75g (3oz) coarse burgul, soaked in
  cold water for 1 hour
4 tablespoons parsley, finely chopped
1 teaspoon cinnamon
1 teaspoon allspice
salt and freshly ground black pepper
300ml (½ pint) tahina sauce
lemon juice to dilute tahina sauce
50g (2oz) pine nuts, slightly browned
  in olive oil

1 Heat the oil in a large, heavy-based frying pan and soften the onions gently. Mix the onion, burgul, herbs, spices and seasoning with the minced lamb. Knead the mixture well. Leave to rest in a cool place for about one hour.

2 Oil a large baking tray and spread the meat mixture into an even flat 2cm (1in) layer. Brush with oil and bake in a pre-heated oven to 180°C, 350°F, gas mark 4, for about 40-45 minutes until the surface is nicely browned.

3 Cover with tahina sauce, diluted with the lemon juice to the consistency of thick cream. Increase the oven temperature to a maximum of 240°C, 460°F, gas mark 9, and bake for approximately ten minutes until the sauce bubbles and starts to brown. Sprinkle the cop of the dish with pine nuts and serve very hot, accompanied with plain boiled rice or a green salad.

Tahina Sauce

Juice of 2 or 3 lemons
250g (8oz) tahina paste
175ml (6fl oz) water
salt
garlic to taste
4 tablespoons parsley, finely chopped

1 Add the lemon juice to the tahina paste and mix well. As you begin to work the tahina paste seems to separate and turn lumpy. Keep mixing, adding in small quantities of water, until the sauce reaches the right consistency. This should resemble the consistency of a thick double cream. Add salt, garlic and parsley to taste.

Brinjal Albaras

Serves 6

45g (1¾oz) creamed coconut or small can of unsweetened coconut milk
5 cloves of garlic
½ hot fresh green chilli pepper, seeded (or more to taste)
2.5cm (1in) fresh ginger
¼ teaspoon ground cloves
½ teaspoon ground cinnamon
½ teaspoon ground turmeric
a good bunch of coriander leaves
salt and freshly ground black pepper to taste
3 tablespoons peanut or light vegetable oil
450g (1lb) onions, cut in 1cm (½in) slices
750g (1½lb) potatoes, cut in 1cm (½in) slices
450g (1lb) aubergines, cut in 1cm (½cm) slices
450g (1lb) tomatoes, cut in 1cm (⅜in) slices

I'd so often felt honoured when treated to sumptuous meals at Claudia Roden's house but this particular day, my joy knew no bounds when the expert herself agreed to cook with me on camera and to show me how to make this aubergine dish. I love aubergines but know few recipes for them, so I welcomed this version of Claudia's, which she describes as 'an extraordinary symphony of flavours' from the Bene Israel of India. And the added bonus is that it is easy to prepare! You need a large, shallow, heavy-bottomed casserole or pot with a tight-fitting lid.

1 Dissolve the creamed coconut (if using) in 100ml (4fl oz) of boiling water. Put the garlic, fresh chilli, ginger, cloves, cinnamon, turmeric, coriander, and a little salt, pepper and the dissolved coconut cream or the canned coconut milk in a food processor and blend to a paste.

2 Dip each vegetable in this paste. Cover the bottom of the casserole or pot with the oil and put in the vegetable slices in layers, beginning with a layer of onions, then potatoes, followed by aubergines and finishing with tomatoes.

3 Put the lid on and cook on very low heat for about an hour, until the vegetables are very soft. They cook in their own juices, turn an earth colour, and become richly imbued with the aromatic flavours.

4 Turn out carefully on a serving platter so that the vegetables remain in layers. Serve hot with bread or chapatis.

Mahasha (Stuffed Vegetables)

serves 6

2 tablespoons vegetable oil plus
    extra for frying
1 teaspoon turmeric
1 large onion, peeled and finely
    chopped
1 teaspoon each of crushed garlic
    and chopped fresh root ginger
2 heaped tablespoons tomato purée
    or paste
250g/8oz minced beef or chicken
1 cup rice, washed and soaked for
    ½ hour, then drained
2 tablespoons chopped, fresh mint
    leaves
250ml (8fl oz water
1 teaspoon brown sugar
½ teaspoon ground coriander
salt and freshly ground black pepper
    to taste
½ cup freshly squeezed lemon juice

The best vegetables to use are large steak tomatoes, small aubergines, medium peppers, cabbage leaves, large onions, vine leaves or cucumbers. If using tomatoes, aubergine, peppers or cucumbers, cut off the tops and retain them, then scoop out and discard the insides. For cabbage, onions and vine leaves, scald them first in boiling water for a few minutes. The outer leaves of the onion are easily removed by cutting from the edge to the centre before scalding. Make a good selection, allowing two per person.

1 Heat two tablespoons of oil and gently fry the turmeric and coriander for thirty seconds. Add the onions, garlic and ginger and sweat for a few minutes, then add the tomato purée. Add the minced meat or chicken and fry gently for two minutes. Put in the rice and stir for about a minute. Turn off the heat and add the mint, toss to mix.

2 Now stuff the vegetables about two-thirds full only to allow space for the rice to swell. Cover with the lids and secure with toothpicks. Place upright in a saucepan in a single layer, arrange fairly tightly together.

3 Add the water with the salt, pepper, sugar and lemon juice. Cover and cook on a medium to low heat for 15–20 minutes or until the rice is cooked and soft.

4 Before serving, shallow fry the stuffed vegetables in hot oil, turning in the pan until browned all over. Remove toothpicks and serve hot.

Fish Kartoffel

450g (1lb) firm medium sized boiling
    potatoes, peeled and quartered
enough gefilte fish stock to cover
    the potatoes
75g (3oz) butter
salt and pepper
sour cream to accompany

Although it is not strictly a fish dish, the following recipe can be made every time Gefilte fish is prepared.

1 Cover the quartered potatoes with the stock, add the butter and season lightly. Bring to the boil and cover.

2 Either simmer very gently on top of the stove or put into a preheated oven at 190°C/375°F/gas mark 5 to cook until most of the liquid is absorbed and the potatoes are beautifully brown and fragrant.

3 Adjust seasoning and serve very hot with a dollop of sour cream.

Gefilte Fish

Serves 6-8

for the stock
heads, bones, trimmings and skin of fish
2 large onions, peeled and sliced into rings
4 large carrots, peeled and sliced into thin rings
4 celery sticks, chopped
water to cover
salt and freshly ground black pepper

for the fish mixture
1½ kg (3lb) mixed filleted fish, at least three kinds (cod, bream, whiting, hake or carp)
2 medium sized onions, peeled and quartered
2-3 tablespoons mild olive or peanut oil
2 eggs, lightly beaten
2 tablespoons ground almonds (optional)
50g (2oz) matzo meal (or use breadcrumbs)
1 medium carrot, peeled and finely grated (optional)
75g (3fl oz) chilled water (for moistening)
2-3 teaspoons salt (this dish takes rather a large quantity of salt)
plenty of freshly ground black pepper

There are literally hundreds of ways of making this popular dish. What is agreed is that the mixture should contain more than one kind of fish – carp is the species which instantly springs to mind, along with sea water fish such as cod, haddock or whiting. The flavour of these fish balls should be intense, the texture light – and the most essential thing, I am told, is that each fish ball *must* be topped with a slice of carrot! In former times the ingredients for the fish balls would be lovingly and laboriously chopped with a blade – nowadays we can use the food processor – or buy the mixture ready made.

1 First make the stock. Rinse the fish heads and trimmings under cold running water, put them into a large stockpot, add the vegetables, cover with cold water and bring to the boil on a high flame. Lower the flame to moderate, skim the stock and simmer gently for 30 minutes. Season with salt and pepper.

2 Meanwhile, to prepare the fish balls, rinse the fillets, pat dry with kitchen paper, remove any stray bones and skin and set aside.

3 Put the onions into the bowl of a food processor, whizz for a few seconds, add the eggs and whizz again to a creamy mixture. Transfer this mixture into a large mixing bowl.

4 Now put the prepared fish into a food processor and pulse for a few seconds – it is very important that the fish is not mushed, just finely minced. Add the fish to the onion and egg mixture and mix in all the remaining ingredients, sprinkling in a little of the chilled water if necessary, to form a fine, homogenous mixture. If the mixture is too soft add some more matzo meal. Cover and leave in the refrigerator for 30 minutes.

5 Shape the mixture into either 4cm (1½in) balls or into torpedo-shaped patties. Slide them into the simmering fish stock, turn the flame to low, and simmer for half an hour to an hour (traditionally gefilte are long-cooked).

6 Use a perforated spoon to lift the fish balls from the stock and arrange on a serving dish. Scoop out the rings of carrot and top each ball with one slice.

7 Boil down the stock to reduce. Strain, cool until almost jellied, spoon over the fish balls and chill.

8 This dish is served cold, accompanied by chrain, a beetroot and horseradish sauce.

Middle Eastern Pizzas

Makes about 15

for the dough

450g (1lb) strong unbleached bread flour, sifted (1 teaspoon reserved)
½ teaspoon salt
50ml (2fl oz) olive oil
10g (½oz) fresh yeast or the recommended equivalent measurement in dried yeast
250ml (8fl oz) tepid water

to finish the pizzas

olive oil for brushing
za'atar or dried oregano

Zahtar or Za'atar is a spicy mixture of wild thyme, roasted sesame seeds, the ground sour red berries of the sumac tree and salt. This popular Israeli spice mixture is available in specialist delis; otherwise your own mixture of herb and sesame seeds could be used.

1 Mix the flour and salt in a large bowl, sprinkle in the oil and rub it through the flour with your fingers.

2 Put the fresh yeast in a small basin, add about two tablespoons of the tepid water, mix to dissolve to a creamy consistency, set aside in a warm place for ten minutes for the yeast to froth (ferment). Follow the packet instructions if using dried yeast.

3 Add the yeast and the remaining tepid water to the flour and use your hands to mix to a soft, unsticky dough. You may have to use a little more or less of the flour or water to achieve this consistency. Knead the dough on a floured working surface for about ten minutes, until the dough is smooth and elastic. Meanwhile wash out the mixing bowl, dry and lightly oil it. Return the ball of dough to the bowl, give it a couple of turns so that the dough is lightly oiled, cover with a damp tea towel and leave to rise until doubled in size – about 2–3 hours.

4 When the dough has risen, preset the oven to 240°C/465°F/gas mark 8/9.

5 Knock down the dough and knead on a lightly floured working surface for one minute. Divide into 50-75g (2-3oz) pieces, rolling each one into a ball between the palms of your hands. Flatten the balls slightly on the working surface and lightly roll to form 0.5cm (¼in) thick rounds. Put these on to one or two baking sheets and gently stub each one with the tips of your fingers so the whole of the surface is covered with small indentations. Brush liberally with olive oil and sprinkle with a generous amount of za'atar or herbs and sesame seeds. Leave to rise in a warm place for 25–30 minutes, by which time the oven will be good and hot for baking.

6 Sprinkle the pizzas with a little cold water. Bake in the oven for five to eight minutes or until they are golden at the edges. Serve hot. The same dough can be made into mini-sized finger food and served with drinks.

Cheturney

5 tablespoons vegetable oil
6 cloves
3 cardamoms
2 cinnamon sticks
1 teaspoon turmeric
2.5cm (1in) root ginger, finely
  chopped
4 cloves garlic, crushed
4 kg (9lb) onions, peeled and finely
  chopped
3 heaped tablespoons tomato purée
2kgs/4lbs fresh tomatoes, peeled
  and chopped
3 red chillies, uncut
salt
juice of 2 fresh lemons

This is a corruption of the Indian word chutney and much influenced by the Indian cuisine of the region. It is slowly cooked but worth the time and effort.

1 In a very large, heavy-based pot, heat up the oil and gently fry all the spices then the ginger and garlic. Add the onions and mix well and allow to sweat. Add the tomato purée, chopped tomatoes, chillies and salt. Cover the pan and cook on high heat for ten minutes.

2 Uncover, turn down heat to the very lowest and cook, stirring from bottom of pan from time to time for up to 6 hours. The cheturney is ready when it is considerably reduced and a deep reddish brown colour. Add the lemon juice and allow to rest overnight.

Mahmoui

Makes around 20

400g (14oz) unsalted butter,
  softened
700g (1½lb) flour
a few drops orange flower water
3-4 tablespoons chilled water
450g (1lb) seedless dates
½ teaspoon ground cardamom
½ teaspoon ground cloves
½ teaspoon ground cinnamon
110g (4oz) extra butter (melted)
icing sugar

This is a truly Sephardi sweet filled with dates or nuts. It was given to me by Aviva Elias, a vibrant woman who lives in London with her equally charismatic father, Moshe. Born in Singapore of Iraqi Jewish parents, Aviva has grown up with a rich heritage of Jewish culinary delights from Iraq, Singapore Chinese, India and Britain and is well poised to share some of hers and her dad's favourite recipes.

1 Line a baking sheet with parchment paper. Pre-heat the oven to 180°C/350°F/gas mark 4. Put the softened butter and flour in a bowl and working with your fingertips, rubbing together until the mixture forms bread crumbs. Add the cold water, one tablespoonful at a time, mixing until a smooth dough is formed. At the same time, add the drops of orange flower water. Divide the dough into 3 balls, wrap in clingfilm and refrigerate for half an hour. Put the dates and spices in a blender with the butter, blend into a smooth paste and refrigerate.

3 Working with one ball at a time, break off a walnut size piece of dough and gradually flatten it in the palm of your hand. Fill with a small nugget of date paste and close to form a ball. Using small tongs or a fork, pinch a pattern on the top and place on a lightly greased baking sheet. Repeat with the remaining dough. Bake the balls for 10–15 minutes. They should not be browned at all, just baked enough to cook the dough. Dust with the icing sugar when cold. These pastries are delicious served with strong Turkish coffee.

Ingberlach

1kg (2lb) carrots, scraped and washed
water or orange juice
sugar
150g (6oz) walnuts, coarsely chopped
1 scant tablespoon ginger

Small carrots are best used for this but adjust the sugar to personal taste.

1 Put the cleaned carrots in a large heavy-based pan, cover with water or orange juice, bring to the boil and simmer until they are soft but not mushy. Drain and allow to cool.

2 Grate the cooked carrots on a fine grater. Squeeze out superfluous moisture and measure the pulp. Allow 250g (8oz) sugar to every 250g (8oz) carrot pulp.

3 Return the pulp to a clean heavy-based pan (a preserving pan is best), add the warmed sugar and bring to the boil. Stir all the time to prevent scorching. When the mixture comes away from the pan sides, whitening in places, stir in the ginger and the nuts.

4 Take off the heat and spread on a wetted board or marble slab. Allow to cool and dry.

5 Cut into neat diamond shapes, turn over and allow to dry on the other side.

6 Store in an airtight tin, with each layer separated with wax paper dusted with sugar.

Orange Cake

Serves 12 or more

2 oranges
6 eggs
250g (9oz) sugar
2 tablespoons orange blossom water
1 teaspoon baking powder
250g (9oz) blanched almonds, coarsely ground

This moist, almost pudding-like Sephardi Orange Cake is one of Claudia Roden's very popular recipes, especially, in Australia. And since my friendship with Claudia started in Australia where we first met, it is fitting that I include this wonderful recipe, with her permission of course! It's like everybody's favourite.

1 Wash the oranges and boil them whole for one and a half hours, or until they are soft.

2 Beat the eggs with the sugar. Add the orange blossom water, baking powder and almonds and mix well.

3 Cut open the oranges, remove the seeds, and purée in a food processor.

4 Mix thoroughly with the egg and almond mixture and pour into a 23cm (9in) oiled cake tin dusted with matzo meal or flour, preferably non-stick with a removable base.

5. Bake in an oven pre-heated to 375°F/190°C/gas mark 5 for an hour. Cool.

Chapter 8: English

A friend of mine said recently that English food is rather like English people: polite, acceptable, not too demanding or dramatic. Well, that's how it looked to me when I came to work in London in the mid-60s. Actually I knew more or less what to expect, on the basis of my encounters with the English in Ghana. For those who start life with English food, it is normal – and most other cuisines are surprisingly spicy and daring. For those moving in the opposite direction, for whom strong flavours are the norm, English food is at first bite (dare I say it?) insipid.

From what I read in the history books, it was not always so. Well, even in the seventeenth century, foreigners were complaining about the English habit of serving salad still wet and not properly dressed, and wondering why people here didn't eat the abundant local mushrooms. But the general picture from the distant past is of market gardens full of garlic, rocket, fennel, celeriac, artichokes and a host of other good things which have only recently reappeared in the shops. Monasteries and great houses had their own walled herb gardens. And the rich at least used to get supplies of all sorts of exotic spices from abroad. What do you think those knights brought back from the Crusades in the Holy Land as presents for their wives? Then the beginnings of the Empire in the reign of Elizabeth I meant that the English were uniquely placed to mix and match flavours from around the world.

There was not only a greater use of herbs and spices. The variety of all sorts of ingredients was tremendous. Accounts of Queen Elizabeth's banquets include asparagus and swan. Even then, chefs travelled abroad to get ideas, though the English had not yet developed their later inferiority complex; menus were still written in English.

Then something seems to have happened to undermine a great cooking heritage. To keep this kind of thing going you need generations of women who have the time and energy to learn and apply the tradition. England had its industrial revolution earlier, quicker and more drastically than other countries. Farming families were uprooted and plonked down in Manchester and Birmingham. Women worked in factories. In the streets on the way home they could grab some fried fish and a piece of bread for themselves and the kids. In the 1870s pommes de terre à la mode arrived from France and were soon renamed ('go down the fish shop and get us a bag of pommes de terre à la mode, will you' just didn't have the right ring to it); combined with the fish, they became one of the first

Swanning it at the Waldorf
Meridien.

classic fast foods. Actually the rot may have set in a hundred years earlier when the Earl of Sandwich. a devoted card-player. couldn't be bothered to break for a proper meal. and ordered up a snack between slices of bread.

I rather fancy that spirit of industry and its benefits may have had a bad effect on eating habits in other ways. Sooner than other nations. the English were converted to the joys of processed food. Sometimes processing disguises things which people would rather not see: people who turn green at the sight of pigs' trotters seem to love them ground up in sausages with all those other less glamorous bits of the animal. City-dwellers get more squeamish by the generation. The story goes that children evacuated from London in the war refused to drink milk on farms because it came from those nasty. muddy cows! Kids who grow up on processed food also miss those indefinable extra flavours and textures when they eat natural food. They don't actually say 'could I have a little emulsifying agent. stabiliser. colour. E101 and antioxidant in this. please?' They just think that auntie can't quite hack it compared to the manufacturers of the micowaveable mini-turkey-kiev-pizzas that they usually get.

If you want fast food. why not go for one of England's greatest glories – cheese? The green fields of England are the dairy cow's heaven. so cheesemakers start with the right stuff. Many of these cheeses are also very cookable. Cauliflower is not a vegetable that works well by itself. but with a straightforward cheese sauce it becomes an understated traditional masterpiece; and the same treatment can be given successfully to lots of other veggies – leeks. carrots. courgettes and more. Check out a slightly more sophisticated version – Leek and Fennel Gratin on page 130.

To keep your crumbly piece of farmhouse Cheddar perfect company. how about a succulent Cox's Orange Pippin or Worcester Parmain? An apple without cheese. they say. is like a kiss without a squeeze. Or maybe glass of real ale? I'm not a great beer drinker. but I can tell that there's a lot more quality and flavour in English bitters than in the light fizzy lager that's taken over the rest of the world. Like red wine. ale gives the best of itself at room temperature – a couple of degrees above zero in most English rooms. Only joking!

Kippers. Lancashire hotpot. roast beef or lamb. summer pudding. Yorkshire pudding. Christmas pudding ... the English actually have lots of great traditional dishes to be proud of. Then there's the game which attracts hunters and gourmets from around the world. And wonderful fish-rich seas. The principle is to treat fine ingredients with a light touch. Take some perfect strawberries. add some perfect cream ... and suddenly you believe that. yes. an English player can win Wimbledon!

Chestnut and Apple Soup

Serves 4

450g (1lb) fresh whole chestnuts or
   a 425g (15oz) tin whole chestnuts
50g (2oz) butter
1 medium onion, peeled and finely
   chopped
1 medium carrot, peeled and very
   finely diced
900ml (1½ pints) vegetable, chicken,
   turkey or pheasant stock
350g (12oz) approximately, eating or
   cooking apples, peeled, cored and
   sliced
sea salt and freshly ground black
   pepper
a pinch of sugar (optional)
a squeeze or two of lemon juice
2-3 tablespoons double cream or
   crème fraîche

to finish
chopped parsley
finely grated lemon rind

to serve
warm wholemeal rolls
slices of Stilton cheese

Christmas – and what to do with all those delicious leftovers. Here's a delicious soup using seasonal ingredients that you're bound to have at hand.

1 If using fresh chestnuts, cut off the pointed ends of the skins and peel. This may be easier by first spreading the chestnuts on a baking sheet and baking in a hot oven for 10 minutes, then peeling when cool enough to handle. Alternatively, drain the tinned chestnuts if using.

2 Melt the butter in a large heavy-based pan on a low to moderate flame, add the onion and carrot to sweat, then add the chestnuts, cover the pan and cook for about 5 minutes, shaking the pan from time to time.

3 Add the stock, turn up the flame and bring up to simmering point. Cook at a gentle simmer for about 30 minutes or until the chestnuts are tender. Add the apples for the last 5 minutes of the cooking time and cook until tender but still whole.

4 Pour the soup into a blender or liquidiser and whizz until smooth. Return the soup to the pan and stir over a low flame. Taste and add the seasonings, using the lemon juice and a pinch of sugar (if using) to balance the taste between tart and sweet, to your preference. Stir in the cream.

5 Ladle into warmed soup bowls, sprinkle with the chopped parsley and finely grated lemon rind. Serve with warm wholemeal rolls and a slice or two of Stilton on the side.

Jayne's Welcome Bread (Brixton Bread)

900g (2lb) organic stoneground
   wholemeal bread flour
2 sachets Easy Blend or Fast Action
   dried yeast
3 teaspoons salt
900ml (1½ pints) or more, tepid
   water to mix

Jayne and I have been friends for 26 years. This is her recipe for bread.

1 Lightly grease two 450g (1lb) loaf tins. Put the dry ingredients into a mixing bowl and combine. Gradually add the water, drawing in the flour and mixing to form a dough. Aim for a soft, pliable, slightly wet dough which you knead for 10 minutes on a lightly floured working surface. Divide the dough in half, shape into oblongs and place in the two prepared loaf tins. Cover the tins with a damp cloth and leave to rise at normal room temperature until doubled in size.

2 Pre-heat the oven to 220°C/425°F/gas mark 7. Bake the loaves in the oven for 30 – 45 minutes until cooked. To test, turn out one of the loaves and lightly tap the underneath; if it sounds hollow then the loaf is cooked. Cool on a wire rack.

English Asparagus – three favourite ways

Serves 4

*20–24 medium asparagus spears,
stems trimmed and peeled if
necessary
110–175g (4–6oz) butter, melted*

to serve
*sea salt and freshly ground black
pepper
a good handful of parsley, finely
chopped
wedges of lemon*

Buy English asparagus in season! Look for young, tightly closed buds, a fresh green colour, and avoid thick fibrous stems with cracked ends. My favourite way to savour the delicate flavour is simply to boil them in the classic way and serve them up with a generous pool of melted butter, sea salt and freshly ground pepper, a squeeze of lemon and a sprinkling of parsley (and finger bowls and spare napkins).

1 Wash the asparagus. If necessary, scrape or peel the lower parts of any thicker stems with a sharp knife. If using a deep pan to cook, make three or four bundles of the asparagus, tying stems together in two places with string, this prevents the tender tips from moving about too much and breaking in the cooking process.

2 Bring a large deep pan of water to the boil, lower the flame to simmering and gently lower in the bundles of asparagus spears. simmer very gently (the cooking time will depend on the size and thickness of the spears).

3 Alternatively, bring about 2.5cm (1in) water to the boil in a very large frying pan, then turn down the flame. Put all of the asparagus in the pan, with all the tips facing in the same direction and place the pan over the flame so that the hottest part of the pan is cooking the stems and the buds are barely simmering.

4 When the asparagus is just tender, lift it out very carefully with a perforated spoon and drain. This is best done flat, on one or two clean tea towels or a wodge of kitchen paper.

5 Serve straight away on warmed dinner plates, with the melted butter in separate pots and with sea salt, the pepper mill, chopped parsley and wedges of lemon to hand.

Variations:
1 To serve cold: plunge the cooked asparagus into cold water for about 30 seconds, then drain well. Arrange on a serving platter and dress the stems with a good home-made vinaigrette flavoured with any of the following: balsamic vinegar, fresh herbs, blanched strips of lemon or orange rind, a squeeze of lime juice, honey and grain mustard. Sprinkle with whole basil leaves to serve.

2 To serve piping hot and roasted: preheat the oven to 240°C/475°F/gas mark 9. Use your hands to swathe the spears in good olive oil and arrange them over the base of a roasting tin. Drizzle over a little more oil, sprinkle with sea salt and freshly ground black pepper and roast in the fierce heat for 10–20 minutes. The spears will shrink somewhat, but the flavour will be stunningly intense. Serve on warmed plates, drizzle over a little more olive oil and cover with shavings of regional English cheese or Parmesan.

Leek and Fennel Gratin

Serves 4–6

2 fat bulbs of fennel, trimmed and
    quartered (green fronds reserved)
700g (1½lb) leeks, trimmed,
    cleaned and cut into 2.5cm (1in)
    rounds or left whole if young,
    including the good green parts
salt

for the cheese sauce
50g (2oz) butter
50g (2oz) plain flour
600ml (1 pint) full cream milk,
    approximately, heated
225–350g (8–12oz) Cheddar cheese,
    grated
pinch salt and freshly ground black
    pepper

for the topping
good handful or two of fresh
    breadcrumbs
50g (2oz) Cheddar cheese, grated
handful of finely chopped almonds
    (optional)
scraps or flakes of butter

to finish
reserved green fennel fronds

This goes particularly well with Parsleyed New Potatoes.

1 First, either steam the vegetables, sprinkling them with a pinch or two of salt, or braise them gently in a little salted water on a moderate flame (reserve the braising liquid to add to the cheese sauce if wished). Do not overcook, the vegetables should be al dente. Drain, set aside and keep warm.

2 Preheat the oven to 200°C/400°F/gas mark 6. Lightly butter a gratin or shallow baking dish.

3 To make the cheese sauce, melt the butter in a medium-sized heavy-based pan on a low flame and whisk in the flour. Cook for about one minute, remove the pan from the flame and let it cool somewhat. Now add the heated milk, whisking continuously, turn up the flame and return the pan to the heat. Simmer the sauce, stirring or whisking constantly until the sauce begins to thicken, then add the cheese and stir until melted. Add a little of the vegetable braising liquid if wished, and continue stirring for about five minutes until the sauce is thick and creamy, or to your liking. Check the taste and add a pinch of salt and pepper accordingly.

4 Arrange the quarters of braised fennel in the dish and intersperse with the whole cooked leeks, or surround the fennel with leek rounds. Coat with the sauce, scatter with the breadcrumbs mixed with the grated cheese and chopped almonds, if using. Strew with a few flakes of butter and bake in the oven for about 10 minutes, until the gratin is golden brown and crisp. Alternatively flash the gratin under a pre-heated hot grill.

5 Scatter over the reserved green fronds of fennel and serve with hot crusty rolls or Parsleyed New Potatoes.

Variation:
For an extra touch, although not entirely English, replace 50–75g (2–3oz) of the Cheddar with grated Parmesan cheese and stir a couple of tablespoons of crème fraîche into the sauce.

Rabbit with Cider in Prunes

Serves 2–3

4 rabbit joints
1 tablespoon seasoned flour
225g (8oz) streaky bacon or
    pancetta (cured spiced belly of
    pork)
1–2 tablespoons sunflower oil
2 large onions, peeled, halved and
    thinly sliced to form crescents
1 clove garlic, peeled and chopped
300ml (10fl oz) cider or dry white or
    red wine
300ml (10fl oz) stock
1 bunch of herbs (bay leaf, parsley,
    thyme)
pinch of salt
freshly ground black pepper
110g (4oz) stoned prunes
whipping or double cream (optional)
knob of butter (optional)

The dry texture of rabbit meat is beautifully complemented by the fruity sauce.

1 First wash the rabbit joints and pat dry with kitchen paper. Dust in seasoned flour and wrap each piece in a strip of bacon or pancetta, securing with cocktail sticks.

2 Heat the oil in a heavy based frying pan and gently cook the onions until brown. Towards the end of their cooking time add the garlic. Transfer to a flameproof casserole and set aside. Brown the rabbit pieces in the frying pan and add these to the casserole.

3 Pour the cider or wine and stock over the rabbit, add the herbs, salt and pepper and gently heat until barely simmering. Cover and continue simmering very gently for 1–1½ hours or until the rabbit is tender. Add the prunes 15 minutes before the time is up.

4 To serve, arrange the rabbit pieces on an attractive shallow platter and keep warm while you quickly boil the sauce to reduce and thicken it. Stir in 1–2 tablespoons of cream or a knob of butter, if using.

5 Pour the sauce all over the rabbit and strew with croûtons and chopped parsley.

Toad in the Hole

Serves 4

for the batter
110g (4oz) plain flour
2 small eggs
pinch salt
300ml (½ pint) milk or half milk
    and half water
handful finely chopped fresh herbs
    or a little finely chopped onion
    (optional)

for the toad
a little oil or poultry dripping
450g (1lb) pork, beef or game
    sausages

For this all-time favourite, find a butcher or food shop which makes or sells really good-quality unadulterated sausages. Braised Red Cabbage (see page 135) and roast onions make excellent accompaniments.

1 In a basin whisk all the ingredients for the batter together until smooth, adding the herbs or a little chopped onion if you wish, and set aside to cool for at least one hour.

2 Preheat the oven to 220°C/425°F/gas mark 7 and light the grill. Put a little oil or dripping into a medium-sized roasting tin and place in the oven. Prick the sausages all over and grill them to partly cook and lose some of their fat for 5–10 minutes, depending on their size and thickness.

3 Take the hot roasting tin from the oven (the oil or dripping should by now be sizzling) and pour in about half the batter mixture so that it sets very slightly. Quickly arrange the sausages on the pudding and pour over the remaining batter.

Slow Roast Pheasant with Braised Red Cabbage

Serves 4-6

1 large or 2 small pheasant
50-75g (2-3oz) butter
110g (4oz) streaky bacon, derinded and diced

for the flavouring vegetables
3-4 shallots, peeled and roughly chopped
1 large carrot, peeled and roughly diced
2-3 stalks celery, scrubbed and finely sliced

for the stock
1-2 teaspoons tomato purée (optional)
freshly ground black pepper
600ml (1 pint) approximately stock or red wine, or half and half
a few sprigs of parsley and a bay leaf

to finish the dish
salt to taste
1-2 tablespoons redcurrant jelly chopped parsley

This is what I call a semi-roast/braise, a simple rustic way of cooking a pheasant (or any game bird) to tenderness when you are uncertain of its age. There is nothing more disappointing than anticipating a delicious supper and finding that your roast pheasant is as tough as old boots!

The braised red cabbage has a long cooking time but loves being re-heated. Neither dish will spoil or overcook by keeping warm.

If you wish, instead of the red cabbage, the carved pheasant would go well with the leek and fennel gratin on page 132 or the winter vegetables on page 90. And creamy mashed potato!

1 Rinse the pheasant and pat dry inside and out with kitchen paper. Set the oven to 180°C/350°F/gas mark 4.

2 Choose a heavy-based casserole dish or deep-sided roasting tin in which the birds will sit quite snugly. Cover the base with the flavouring vegetables.

3 Melt the butter in a large heavy-based frying pan on a moderate flame, fry the bacon gently until the fat runs, scoop out with a perforated spoon and transfer to the casserole. Brown the pheasant in the pan and put breast-side down in the casserole.

4 Pour some of the stock or wine into the frying pan and stir to deglaze, stirring in the tomato purée if using, and add to the casserole. Top up with more stock or wine to cover the vegetables by about 2.5-5cm (1-2in). Add pepper, push in the herbs, cover the dish, bring to simmering point and put in the oven for about one to two hours. The cooking time will depend on the size and age of the birds; approximately half way through the cooking time, turn the pheasant breast-side up and baste.

5 Transfer the cooked pheasant to a warmed dish, cover and keep warm. the cooking liquid may now be strained and quickly boiled to reduce somewhat, with the addition of 1-2 tablespoons of redcurrant jelly and seasoning to taste. Alternatively spoon the cooking liquid and vegetables into the bowl of a blender or liquidiser and purée, add redcurrant jelly and seasoning to taste to create a creamy textured flavoursome gravy.

Braised Red Cabbage

900g (2lb) red cabbage, outer leaves and core removed and finely shredded across the grain
450g (1lb) onion, peeled and finely sliced
450g (1lb) cooking apples, peeled, cored and sliced
1-2 handfuls raisins
3 tablespoons brown sugar
½ teaspoon ground cloves
1 teaspoon ground cinnamon
1-1½ teaspoons freshly grated nutmeg
salt and freshly ground pepper to taste
3-4 tablespoons wine vinegar
25-50g (1-2oz) butter

1 Preset the oven to 150°C/300°F/gas mark 2.

2 Layer the cabbage, onions, apples and raisins in a very large heavy-based casserole, sprinkling the layers with the sugar, spices and seasonings. Pour in the wine vinegar, flake the butter over the top and cover the pan with a tight fitting lid – if necessary use a sheet of aluminium foil under the lid to make a tight seal. Bring the casserole up to just under simmering point on a moderate flame, then transfer to the oven.

3 Braise the cabbage for two to three hours until meltingly soft and tender and infused with the spices. Stir once during the cooking time.

To serve: arrange servings of the braised red cabbage on warmed dinner plates, accompanied with portions of the carved pheasant and sauce. Serve with potatoes if wished, and redcurrant jelly.

Traditional Roast Beef and Yorkshire Pudding

There are many approaches to roasting a joint of beef. Some cooks like to put the joint in the pre-heated oven at maximum heat and give it a good blast for ten to twenty minutes, before turning off the oven and leaving it to cook in its own heat – usually resulting in a succulent rare-ish roast – but this takes a bit of practice. Other cooks swear by roasting at a low temperature so that the meat is cooked evenly throughout. Here is a way to cook a traditional family English roast, producing a joint which is crispy outside and which can be from rare to well done to your taste, to serve with Yorkshire puddings and horseradish sauce. It is lovely just simply served with the meat juices, but I have given the method for a traditional gravy if preferred. Small joints tend to shrink when roasted, so it is worth cooking a larger joint than needed for best results and wonderful cold slices for the next day.

Make sure that you let the joint stand at room temperature for one or two hours before roasting.

**Serves at least 6
(allow approximately 175-225g
(6-8oz) raw meat weight per
person)**

1.8-2.3kg (4-5lb) joint of rolled
  sirloin, boned rolled rib or topside
salt to taste
½ onion, unpeeled
1 carrot, peeled and roughly
  chopped

for the roast potatoes
700-900g (1½-2lb) potatoes
1 onion, peeled and sliced in half
freshly ground black pepper
coarse sea salt

for the Yorkshire Pudding
see following recipe

for the gravy (optional)
reserved vegetable stock
1 tablespoon flour, approximately
salt and freshly ground black pepper

to serve
a selection of root vegetables, such
as parsleyed carrots, parsnips, baby
turnips, or steamed greens.

1 Pre-heat the oven to 230°C/450°F/gas mark 8. Wipe the joint with a dampened piece of kitchen paper. Prick the fat with a fork and rub salt all over the fat to produce a crispy crust. Put the joint in a heavy roasting tin, tucking the unpeeled half onion and chopped carrot under the meat; they will slightly caramelise and absorb some of the meat fats and help to make a flavoursome gravy. Roast in the very hot oven for approximately 15 minutes to seal and crisp the meat, then turn down the heat to 180°C/350°F/gas mark 4. Continue roasting, allowing approximately 12-15 minutes per 450g (1lb) meat for rare, 15-18 minutes for medium and 20-25 minutes for a well-done roast. A simple method of testing for doneness if you do not have a meat thermometer is to insert a metal skewer into the middle of the joint and leave it for half a minute. When you pull the skewer out, if it is cold then the meat is not cooked; if it is warm, the meat will be rare and if it is hot then the meat is cooked right through.

2 Meanwhile peel the potatoes and cut into roasting size. Boil in a large pan of salted water with the two halves of onion for about ten minutes or until half cooked. Drain through a colander over a bowl, reserving the cooking water for the gravy. Remove the onion. Return the potatoes to the hot pan and let them dry in the steam for a minute. Scrape them gently with a fork – this will make really crispy potatoes. Set aside.

3 Transfer the joint into a warmed serving plate, tent loosely with aluminium foil and put to rest in a warm place.

4 Pour a little fat from the roasting tin into a clean pan, add the potatoes and quickly turn them in the sizzling fat. Sprinkle over pepper and sea salt and put in the oven turned up to 220°C/425°F/gas mark 7 for 50-60 minutes.

5 About half way through the cooking time for the roast potatoes, cook the Yorkshire puddings (see following recipe).

6 Meanwhile cook a selection of root vegetables and/or greens, saving the cooking water for making the gravy. Keep the vegetables warm in covered warmed serving dishes.

7 To make the gravy, pour off excess fat from the joint roasting tin and put the tin on a low to moderate flame. Remove the onion skin and mash down the softened onion and carrot. Add approximately one tablespoon of flour and stir well, scraping up all the meaty bits from the bottom of the pan. Cook the roux until it is dark brown, remove the pan from the heat and gradually whisk in enough reserved vegetable water until a smooth gravy is created. Put the pan back on the heat and keep stirring until the gravy thickens, add the meat juices from the joint, taste and season, pour into a jug, and keep warm.

8 Take the joint to the table for carving. Use a perforated spoon to transfer the roast potatoes to a warmed serving dish, surround them with the individual Yorkshire puddings and take these to the table with the dishes of vegetables, the jug of gravy and make sure there is a nice dish of creamed horseradish sauce to hand.

Yorkshire Pudding

Serves: This batter is for making individual Yorkshire Puddings in patty tins; the quantity makes about 12.

75g (3oz) plain flour
pinch salt
1 egg
75ml (3fl oz) milk
75ml (3fl oz) water
Dripping from the roast, good beef or pork dripping, lard or vegetable oil

1 Put all the ingredients for the pudding into a mixing bowl and use a whisk or electric hand mixer to beat the ingredients into a smooth batter. When well mixed there should be tiny bubbles on the surface of the batter.

2 Pre-set the oven to 220°C/425°F/gas mark 7.

3 Put a little knob of dripping or some drops of vegetable oil into the patty tins and put the tray in the pre-heated oven for about 10 minutes. until the dripping or oil is very hot – to smoking point. Pour the batter into the patty tins – try to do this quickly. retaining the heat. so that the batter sizzles and seizes as it hits the hot fat – and straight away return the dish to the oven. Cook for between 15 and 20 minutes and do not open the oven door for the first ten minutes. Serve immediately.

Steak and Kidney Pie

Serves 6

for the pastry
use 1 packet shortcrust pastry, defrosted or make your own:
180g (6oz) plain flour
pinch salt
70g (2¼oz) butter
25g (1oz) lard
2-3 tablespoons iced water
salt and pepper

for the filling
700g (1½lb) stewing steak, trimmed and cubed
225g (8oz) kidneys, trimmed, cored and cut in slices
3 tablespoons flour, seasoned
50g (2oz) butter
1 onion, peeled and sliced
450ml (¾pint) beef stock
2 tablespoons dark ale
parsley and thyme
salt and freshly ground black pepper

for the glaze
1 egg yolk mixed with a little milk

1 Sift the flour and salt together and rub in the fats. You can use a food processor. Add the seasoning. then the iced water to mix to a soft. pliable dough. Sprinkle with flour. cover with clingfilm and leave in the refrigerator to relax for one hour before rolling out.

2 For the filling. wash the meats and pat dry with kitchen paper. Put the seasoned flour into a large. polythene bag with the meats and shake gently to coat. Melt the butter in a heavy-based frying pan on a medium heat and cook the onions and mushrooms for three minutes. Add the steak and kidney and stir well. Cook until lightly browned. Add the stock. ale and herbs and simmer. covered. on low heat for about one hour.

3 Pre-heat the oven to 200°C/400°F/gas mark 6. Lightly grease a pie dish and pour in the steak and kidney mixture. Remove the pastry from the refrigerator and roll out on a clean. lightly floured work surface to a thickness of 0.5cm (1/4in). Place an egg cup upside down in the middle of the meat mixture. It should keep the pastry from touching the surface of the meat. Carefully drape the pastry over the top of the dish to completely cover. Trim round the edges with a knife. Collect the excess pastry together. roll out and cut your favourite fancy shapes to decorate the top of the pie. Lightly moisten with water to stick on the pattern. Paint the top of the pie with the glaze and bake in the oven for 45 minutes until lightly browned. This should smell wonderfully rich and tempting!

Fish and Chips

Serves 4

*4 fillets of any firm white fish, e.g.
    cod, haddock, plaice, skate wings
juice of ¹/₂ lemon
freshly ground black pepper
a little seasoned flour
vegetable oil for shallow frying*

for the batter
*225g (8oz) flour
good pinch salt
1 teaspoon baking powder
300ml (¹/₂ pint) water*

for the chips
*4 large potatoes, peeled
pinch sea salt and freshly ground
black pepper (optional)
vegetable oil for deep frying*

to serve
malt vinegar or wedges of lemon

1 Wash the fish fillets and pat dry with kitchen paper. Sprinkle with a little lemon juice and pepper.

2 Put the batter ingredients into a mixing bowl, whisk together and set aside.

3 Cut the potatoes into chips, heat the oil in a pan suitable for deep-frying to 325°C/160°F. Lower the chips into the oil and fry for 5–6 minutes until they are just beginning to turn pale brown. Lift them out of the oil, drain and leave them to cool. At this stage, if wished, sprinkle the chips with the optional salt and freshly ground black pepper and give them a good toss. This is for flavour and extra crispness. Now raise the temperature of the oil to 375°C/190°F. Deep fry the chips again at the higher temperature for about 2 minutes until they are crisp and brown.

4 Meanwhile, in a large heavy-based deep-sided frying pan heat up about 2.5cm (1in) oil for frying the fish. Dredge the fillets of fish with the seasoned flour, dip in the batter to coat, and shallow fry in the hot oil for about 2–3 minutes on each side, depending on the thickness of the fillets. Drain on crumpled kitchen paper. Serve the fish and chips straight away on warmed plates.

Dover Sole with Butter and Lemon

Serves 2–4

*2–4 Dover sole
75g (3oz) butter
a little milk
50g (2oz) flour
pinch of salt and freshly ground
    black pepper
juice of ¹/₂ lemon
1–2 tablespoons finely chopped
    parsley to garnish
wedges of lemon*

Leave the heads and skin on the fish, if possible. If you prefer, you can take off the dark skin, but leave the white skin on as it becomes deliciously crisp and also helps keep the shape of the fish. Boiled new potatoes, buttered and parsleyed, make a good accompaniment.

1 Wash the fish and pat it dry with kitchen paper. Heat up half the butter in a frying pan. Dip the soles in the milk, then in the flour (seasoned with salt and pepper) in a swift, light flowing action. Fry the soles for 4–5 minutes on each side, according to the thickness of the fish. Transfer them to warmed plates and keep warm.

3 The butter used for cooking the soles should now be golden brown. Now add the remaining butter and the lemon juice, swirl it around the pan, scraping up all the fishy juices and pour this sauce over the soles.

4 Scatter with the finely chopped parsley before serving. (Sole is nice served on the bone but if you prefer you can easily lift off the fillets just before serving.)

Strawberries with a Rose-Scented Cream

900g (2lb) strawberries, rinsed and
   hulled
50–75g (2–3oz) caster sugar, to taste

for the cream
1 egg white
25g (1oz) caster sugar
200ml (7fl oz) crème fraîche
2 tablespoons double cream
half quantity of English Custard
   made with the addition of one egg
   yolk, cooled
2 drops essence of rosewater

to serve
slices of Shortbread (see page 111),
red rose petals, if available

**A recipe idea passed on to me by a friend, a stalwart of the weekly produce
and home-cooking market of the local Women's Institute.**

1 Put the prepared strawberries into a large, pretty glass bowl, sprinkle with sugar to
taste, mix gently and set aside.

2 Whisk the egg white until stiff, adding the sugar half way through the whisking
process. Put the crème fraîche, double cream and custard into a mixing bowl and beat
together. Stir in the essence of rosewater to taste. Use a metal spoon to fold in the egg
white. Chill.

3 Just before serving, top the strawberries with the chilled cream, scatter with red
rose petals, if available, and serve with the slices of Shortbread.

Gingernuts

Makes 14–16 biscuits

110g (4oz) plain flour
1 teaspoons ground ginger to taste
½ teaspoon mixed ground spices
1 teaspoon bicarbonate of soda
50g (2oz) butter
50g (2oz) sugar
50g (2oz) or 2-2½ tablespoons
   golden syrup

1 Lightly butter two or three baking sheets and preheat the oven to 190°C/375°F/
gas mark 5.

2 Sieve the flour, spices and bicarbonate of soda into a mixing bowl, add the sugar
and rub in the butter between your fingers and thumbs until the mixture resembles
fine breadcrumbs. Stir in the golden syrup and mix thoroughly to a thick stiffish
paste.

3 Take pieces of the mixture, each about the size of a walnut, roll into ball shapes
between your hands, and arrange on the prepared baking sheets, allowing space
around them to flatten and spread as they cook. Bake in the oven for about 12–15
minutes until golden brown. Cool on the baking sheets for about one minute, then
transfer the still softish biscuits to wire racks to finish cooling and become crisp and
biscuity.

Chapter 9: Italian

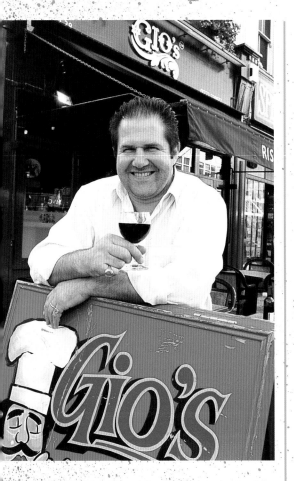

The Italians have rarely had an image problem in these islands. They're seen as stylish, musical, great cooks – and they're even good at football. For some reason I've never understood, half of Shakespeare's plays seem to be set in Italy. And your Byrons, Shelleys and Brownings couldn't keep away from the place.

There has been an Italian community in Britain for a long time, especially around Clerkenwell and Holborn in the City of London, where a veritable 'Little Italy' grew up in the nineteenth century. This was the centre of the ice-cream trade, which had real Italian roots – it was first made using ice from Mount Etna in Sicily. Street musicians and dancers, vendors and artisans were all based in this small cluster of streets around St Peter's Italian church. (The church is still there, and there is a big procession for Our Lady of Mount Carmel in July; but sadly the area has been given over to office blocks.)

England was a haven for political exiles before Italy was freed from foreign rule and unified in 1870. Mazzini, who inspired the liberation struggle, lived in London and set up a school in Hatton Garden. When Garibaldi, who had led the fight against the French and Austrians, visited in 1864, he had a rapturous reception the like of which wasn't seen again until Nelson Mandela came to London. He even had a biscuit named after him, known endearingly as 'squashed flies'!

Of course Britain used to be much more industrialised than Italy, so people came for jobs – to Glasgow, South Wales and odd spots like Bedford where there's a consulate and almost a quarter of a million people of Italian origin. Some came to get away from fascism before the last war; they later suffered the indignity and injustice of being interred by the British government when the war started. Then there were prisoners of war in camps dotted around the country. Italians were put to work on surrounding farms and some made very good friends with the owners (or their daughters!) and stayed on to work largely in the food industry.

Italians in Britain have tended not to stick together in their own little areas, less so anyway than say the Greek Cypriots. Italians shared their churches with Irish and Polish communities, and English catholics. Also they came from many different parts of Italy – many but not all from the poorer south and from Sicily. Those in South Wales mostly trace their origins to Liguria, these days one of the richest corners of Europe.

In the history of foreign food in Britain, Italians have a very special place. In the 50s and 60s they were the first to break through that brittle outer layer of prejudice. They established the trend by which the British accepted, and little by little embraced, the exotic. It all started with a small cup of espresso coffee. Then came maybe a salami sandwich, then a slice of pizza and plate of spaghetti bolognese. The next thing they knew, the British were knocking back sun-dried tomatoes, rocket and artichoke hearts; drenching their salads in balsamic vinegar and virgin olive oil, buying ready-to-bake ciabatta, and strewing basil all over the place!

The Italian restaurant is an essential feature of most towns in Britain, from a little trattoria in a Welsh pit village to the costly marvels of Antonio Carluccio's Neal Street Restaurant and the ultra-fashionable River Café. And don't forget (how could you?) pizza. Long before the hamburger muscled in on the scene, the Neapolitans were perfecting the simple but brilliant fast-food formula that was to become the world's most popular portable meal-in-one. Not that it's fast to make: if you start from scratch, it's actually a couple of hours' work (don't let that put you off, though!)

Pasta, considered just a little bit sophisticated when I first lived in London, has ended up as what every British mum gives her kids, in the sure knowledge that, though there may be quibbles about the sauce, no child ever turns down a plate of spaghetti. And very good, healthy food it is, too. In fact Italian cuisine in general has been given the seal of approval by the dieticians. So get working on these recipes, and buon appetito!

Fratelli Camisa in Soho.

Bruschetta Rustica

Serves 5

3 large peppers, green, red and
  yellow, cored and deseeded
2 tablespoons olive oil,
  approximately
handful parsley, finely chopped
1 clove garlic, crushed, peeled and
  very finely hashed
sea salt and freshly ground black
  pepper
1–2 sticks French bread, cut into 30
  1cm (½in) slices

to finish
whole basil leaves

A popular appetiser – colourful, very moreish and absolutely delicious served with a dish of olives and perhaps a few slices of Parma ham.

1 Preheat the oven to 220°C/425°F/gas mark 7.

2 Put the peppers into a baking tin and roast in the oven, turning occasionally, until the skins are scorched and blistered – about 30-40 minutes. The roasting process gives a concentrated roasted flavour and tender juicy flesh.

3 As soon as the peppers are cool enough to handle, peel away the skins and dice the flesh. Mix with the olive oil, parsley, garlic and salt and pepper to taste, to form a coarse-textured mixture.

4 Toast both sides of the slices of French bread to a light golden brown, top with the pepper mixture and serve immediately.

Risotto Primavera

Serves 10

5-6 tablespoons olive oil
1 onion, peeled and finely chopped
3 large peppers, green, yellow and
  red, deseeded, cored and finely
  chopped
50g (2oz) fresh or frozen green peas
900g (2lb) arborio rice
½ glass vino bianco (dry white wine)
1.6 litres (2¼ pints) vegetable or light
  chicken stock, heated to simmering
  point in a separate pan
110g (4oz) butter, diced
110g (4oz) Parmesan, freshly grated
salt and freshly ground black pepper

1 In a very large heavy-based pan heat the olive oil on a moderate flame and fry the onion gently until soft and transparent. Add the peppers, peas and rice and continue to cook for two minutes.

2 Pour in the wine, stir and cook for a further three or four minutes.

3 Now begin to add the hot stock, a ladleful at a time. As the rice begins to absorb the stock, add another ladleful of hot stock. Continue this process, adding the stock as the rice cooks and absorbs each ladleful until the rice is cooked – usually about 20-25 minutes. Test the rice; it should be just between tender and firm to the bite. The texture of the risotto should be creamy – not too liquid or soupy and not too dry and stodgy.

4 During the last two minutes of cooking add the butter and parmesan and stir gently to fold and melt into the risotto.

5 Take the risotto to the table and serve into warmed shallow soup plates.

Risotto alle Nonne

Serves 6

450g (1lb) cooked prawns
700g (1½lb) salmon, skinned and
boned
1.1 litres (2 pints), approximately,
light vegetable stock, heated to
simmering point in a separate pan
5 tablespoons olive oil
1 onion, peeled and finely chopped
350g (12oz) arborio rice
1–2 tablespoons cream
50g (2oz) Parmesan cheese, freshly
grated
ruccola lettuce leaves, sliced into thin
ribbons
salt and freshly ground black pepper
to taste

Arborio rice is essential for making risotto and now quite widely available in supermarkets and food stores. Also essential is a very large heavy-based pan – the rice will increase considerably in volume as the stock is added. The salmon and prawns are interchangeable with other varieties of fresh fish or shellfish, but the results will be disappointing if frozen seafood is used – the same goes for the Parmesan; buy a nice fresh piece for grating and avoid the powdery ready-grated stuff!

1 Peel the prawns and set aside. Put the heads and shells into a pan, cover with water, boil on a moderate flame for about ten minutes, strain and press slightly in a sieve over a bowl and pour this cooking liquid into the hot vegetable stock. Keep the pan at just under simmering point.

2 Rinse the salmon and pat dry on kitchen paper, check for any stray bones and cut into chunks.

3 In a very large heavy-based pan, heat the olive oil on a moderate flame and fry the onion gently until soft and transparent. Add the rice, toast briefly, stirring so all the grains are glistening and coated in the oil.

4 Now begin to add the hot stock, a ladleful at a time. As the rice begins to absorb the stock add another ladleful of hot stock. Continue this process, gradually adding the stock as the rice cooks and absorbs each ladleful, until the rice is al dente – usually about 20–25 minutes. No more than five minutes before the end of the cooking time, gently fold in the prawns and salmon.

5 Stir in the cream, Parmesan and lettuce ribbons and stir gently to fold and melt into the risotto. Finally season to taste, bearing in mind that the fish and cheese are already quite salty.

6 Take the Risotto to the table and serve into warmed shallow soup plates.

Funghi Ripieni

Serves 10

10 medium open mushrooms, stalks
  removed and reserved

for the stuffing
1-2 tablespoons Italian olive oil
½ medium sized onion, peeled and
  very finely chopped
2 cloves garlic, crushed, peeled and
  very finely hashed
reserved mushroom stalks, finely
  chopped
110-175g (4-6oz) pork, minced
freshly ground black pepper
½ glass vino bianco (dry white
  wine)
pinch or two of salt to taste
110g (4oz) fresh breadcrumbs,
  approximately
1 egg, beaten
110-175g (4-6oz) cheese, grated
  (1 tablespoon reserved)
2 handfuls parsley, finely chopped
  (1 tablespoon reserved)
a little seasoned flour
oil for frying

For these stuffed mushrooms, use open cultivated mushrooms – of course the amount of the stuffing will vary slightly according to the size of the mushrooms.

1 Wipe the mushrooms with dampened kitchen paper and remove the stalks. Chop the stalks finely and reserve for the stuffing ingredients.

2 Now make the stuffing. Put the olive oil into a medium sized heavy-based pan on a low to moderate flame, add the onion and sweat gently for a few minutes. Add the garlic and continue cooking for two or three more minutes until the onion and garlic are soft and transparent but not browned.

3 Add the minced pork and finely chopped mushroom stalks, season with the pepper and stir and fry until the pork takes some colour and the stalks are soft. Add the wine and a pinch or two of salt and cook gently for ten minutes, or until the wine has almost evaporated. Transfer this mixture to a mixing bowl and allow to cool.

4 Add the breadcrumbs, egg and cheese to the cooled stuffing mixture and stir well to combine. It should be a firm but moist mixture; add a few more breadcrumbs if necessary. Stuff the mixture into the mushrooms and coat with a little seasoned flour.

5 Heat the oil in a heavy-based pan suitable for deep frying on a moderate flame. Lower the stuffed mushrooms into the pan, and fry for 1–2 minutes, until golden brown. Remove from the pan with a perforated spoon, and drain on crumpled kitchen paper.

6 Arrange the mushrooms on a serving platter, sprinkle with the reserved chopped parsley and serve warm.

Cipolla al Agrodolce

Serves 6

900g (2lb) pickling onions, peeled
3–4 tablespoons olive oil
water to cover
pinch of salt, to taste
2–3 tablespoons granulated sugar
55–75ml (2–3fl oz) red wine vinegar

A tempting antipasto dish of sweet and sour baby onions. Alternatively they can be served cold with salads, or warm as an accompaniment to meat dishes.

1 Put the peeled onions into a very large heavy-based pan, add the olive oil, enough water just to cover and a pinch of salt.

2 Bring to a gentle simmer on a moderate flame, cover the pan and continue cooking until the onions are tender and the liquid has evaporated.

3 Now stir in the sugar to taste and the red wine vinegar, cover the pan and continue cooking for a few more minutes. Remove the lid from the pan and shake and cook the onions for a final minute or two, or until all the remaining liquid has evaporated. Serve warm or cold.

Bragiolini di Pepperoni

Serves 2

3–4 large peppers, green, red and
  yellow
1–2 tablespoons groundnut oil
2–3 handfuls of soft breadcrumbs
50–110g (2–4oz) Pecorino cheese
1 clove garlic, crushed, peeled and
  very finely chopped
handful of basil leaves, to taste,
  roughly chopped
1–2 teaspoons capers, to taste,
  chopped

to finish
a few basil leaves

Juicy pepper rolls around an arresting filling – this is very much a hands-on recipe in which approximate quantities are given for stuffing, as the amount used will depend upon the size of the peppers. Allow one to two peppers per person.

1 Wipe the peppers. Cut them lengthways into four. Deseed and cut out the core.

2 Heat the oil in a medium-sized heavy-based pan on a low to moderate flame, add the peppers, cover the pan and sweat them gently until they are tender and the skins have shrunk and softened, but do not brown them. This takes about 20 minutes, by which time the peppers will have exuded juices and flavour into the oil.

3 Drain the peppers through a sieve over a bowl, reserving the oil, and allow both peppers and oil to cool. Carefully slip off the skins and lay the peppers on the working surface.

4 Stir in the breadcrumbs to the flavoured cooled oil, adding just enough to absorb all the oil and soften. Mix in the Pecorino, garlic and basil.

5 Spoon a little of the mixture on to each piece of pepper and sprinkle over the capers. Roll up each pepper, arrange on serving dish, seam side down, garnish with basil leaves and serve.

Matribologna

Serves 10

for the Ragù Bolognese (this can be prepared ahead of time)

450g (1lb) best quality chuck steak, minced
25g (1oz) butter
3 tablespoons Italian olive oil
50g (2oz) pancetta or bacon, de-rinded and diced
1 small onion, peeled and finely chopped
1 small carrot, peeled and finely diced
1 stick celery, trimmed and finely chopped
1 clove of garlic, crushed, peeled and finely chopped
150ml (5fl oz) red wine
150ml (5fl oz) chicken or beef stock
1 x 400g (14oz) tin tomatoes, roughly chopped and juice reserved
1 tablespoon tomato purée
pinch or two of salt
freshly ground black pepper

to cook the Matribologna
50g (2oz) butter
400g (14oz) pancetta or bacon, de-rided and diced
350g (12oz) mushrooms, stemmed, wiped with dampened kitchen paper, sliced
110g (4oz) Parmesan, freshly grated
275g (10oz) Ragù Bolognese
120ml (4fl oz) double cream
1kg (2¼lb) Rigatoni or Conchiglie

to finish the dish
1-2 tablespoons Parmesan, freshly grated
basil leaves

Gio's restaurant has a special way of bringing together this classic pasta dish. First a quantity of the sauce is slowly cooked to produce the characteristic velvety textured Ragù Bolognese. Then, at the last moment, a mixture of chopped bacon, mushrooms, cream and parmesan is gently pan fried to add to the sauce and pasta – and believe me it's meraviglioso!!

(The ragù can be prepared a day or two in advance if you like – it's a good idea to make a large quantity which can be frozen for future use for layering lasagne, mixing with macaroni, and many other pasta dishes.)

1 First make the Ragù Bolognese. Heat the butter and oil in a heavy-based pan, add the bacon, carrot and celery and sweat over a low flame until all the vegetables are soft. Turn up the flame a little and add the beef and garlic. Continue to cook, stirring all the time to spread the meat around the pan, until it has taken some colour.

2 Now turn up the flame to moderate, pour in the wine and stock, bring to the boil, and cook until liquid has almost vanished. Stir in the tomatoes and juice and tomato puree, season to taste, turn the flame to low and cook, uncovered, at just under simmering point for at least 1½–2½ hours, stirring occasionally. The longer the cooking time, the smoother the sauce will be. The sauce may now be cooled and kept in the refrigerator for one or two days.

3 To cook the Matribologna, bring a very large pan of salted water to the boil on a high flame, add a drop or two of olive oil to prevent the pasta sticking together, tip in the penne, bring back to the boil, turn down the flame to moderate and boil for approximately eight minutes or according to the instructions on the packet. When the pasta is al dente, drain and return to the hot pan with one tablespoon of the cooking water – this will keep the pasta moist and enhance the flavour of the sauce. Cover and keep warm.

4 Melt the butter in a large heavy-based frying pan on a low to moderate flame, add the bacon and cook until the fat runs, then add the mushrooms and continue frying until the bacon is just crispy and the mushrooms are soft.

5 Tip in 275g (10oz) of the Ragù Bolognese, add the cream, stir in the Parmesan and mix well. Tip into the pan of pasta and mix well.

6 Serve the Matribologna in warmed shallow pasta bowls with a sprinkling of freshly grated Parmesan and roughly torn basil leaves to garnish.

Penne oll'Ortolana

Serves 10

for the pasta
1kg (2¼lb) penne

for the sauce
2-3 tablespoons extra virgin olive oil
1 onion, peeled and finely chopped
2 cloves garlic, crushed, peeled and
　finely chopped (optional)
110g (4oz) pancetta or smoked
　streaky bacon rashers, diced
3 peppers, red, yellow and green,
　quartered, deseeded and sliced
1-2 courgettes, trimmed, sliced in
　half lengthways and chopped
1 aubergine, trimmed and diced
½ glass vino bianco (dry white wine)
1kg (2¼lb) ripe tomatoes, peeled,
　deseeded and diced
4 tablespoons cream
salt and freshly ground black pepper
110g (4oz) Parmesan, freshly grated

garnish
a few basil leaves and an extra
　grating of Parmesan

Find your best huge serving bowl to serve this gorgeous pasta dish for a party of ten. Serve with a crisp mixed green salad and vino.

1　Heat the oil in a large heavy-based pan on a moderate heat and fry the onion and pancetta gently until the fat begins to run. Add the garlic, and cook until the onion is soft and transparent. Add the peppers, courgette and aubergine and fry gently for two or three minutes. Pour in the wine and cook until all the vegetables are tender.

2　To peel the tomatoes, plunge them into boiling water for a few seconds, pierce with a sharp knife and skin. Cut in half and squeeze out the pips, then dice the flesh. Stir the tomato into the pan of vegetables with the cream and season with salt and freshly ground black pepper to taste. Cook until heated through and amalgamated.

3　Meanwhile bring a very large pan of salted water to the boil, add a drop or two of olive oil to prevent the pasta sticking together, tip in the penne, and cook according to instructions on the packet. When the pasta is al dente, drain and tip the sauce over the pasta, then add the Parmesan cheese and stir well to combine.

4　Pour the Penne oll'Ortolana into a warmed serving bowl, garnish with basil leaves and Parmesan and serve immediately.

Involtini di Vitello

Serves 1

1 escalope of veal, preferably topside
2–4 slices prosciutto (Parma ham)
1 tablespoon Parmesan cheese,
　freshly grated
1–2 tablespoons seasoned flour
2 tablespoons olive oil
10g (scant ½oz) butter

A veal dish for one. Would be nice served with baby new potatoes and courgettes, buttered and parsleyed, or drizzled with olive oil.

1　Wash the veal and pat dry with kitchen paper. Cut in half and place between two sheets of greaseproof paper or clingfilm. Use a wooden rolling pin or pounder, and beat them to flatten. Cover each with the slices of prosciutto, trimming to make a neat fit. Sprinkle with the cheese. Roll up each escalope, coat lightly with a little seasoned flour and secure the rolls with wooden cocktail sticks.

3　Heat up the olive oil in a small heavy-based frying pan on a moderate flame and fry the Involtini on one side for three minutes, then turn and cook for a further two minutes. Turn the flame down slightly, add the butter and cook for a final two minutes. Serve immediately with the buttery meat juices from the pan drizzled over.

Rombo al Limone

Serves 2–3

1 chicken turbot, gutted
salt and freshly ground white pepper
2 tablespoons olive oil
1 clove garlic
½ glass vino bianco (dry white
  wine)
juice of lemon
a little vegetable stock
50g (2oz) butter, diced and chilled

to serve
thin slices of lemon
wedges of lemon

Turbot is a top fish, and quite delicious baked, as here. Small ones, when available, are known as chicken turbot and will usually weigh between 900g and 1½kg (2–3lb); enough for two to three servings, bearing in mind that the head of the fish weighs heavy and, by the way, makes excellent fish stock.

1 Rinse the fish and pat dry with kitchen paper. Score two or three diagonal cuts on each side of the fish and season with a little salt and freshly ground white pepper.

2 When ready to cook, pre-heat the oven to 190°C/375°F/gas mark 5.

3 Drizzle a little of the olive oil into a very large roasting tin or a large frying pan with an ovenproof handle. Put the turbot into the pan and tuck in the clove of garlic alongside, to flavour the fish and scent the oil. Drizzle over the remaining olive oil and the lemon juice and add the wine to the pan.

4 Bake in the oven. After 10–15 minutes, check whether the fish is done. The flesh is very firm, quickly turns white and eases from the bone when just cooked; test with a soft-bladed knife in one of the cuts in the fish. Do not overcook the fish and bear in mind that the flesh on the bone continues to cook when removed from the oven and kept warm.

5 When the fish is done, use two spatulas to transfer it carefully to a warmed serving platter, cover with aluminium foil and keep warm.

6 To make the sauce, put the roasting pan containing the fishy cooking juices on to a moderate flame, add a little vegetable stock and cook at a fast simmer for about one minute to reduce somewhat. Remove the garlic. Check the seasoning at this stage, adding salt and pepper and a squeeze or two more lemon juice if necessary. Finally whisk in the cubes of chilled butter to give a glossy finish to the sauce.

7 To serve, pour a little of the sauce over the turbot, arrange a few thin slices of lemon on the fish and take to the table straight away, with the remaining sauce and wedges of lemon to be handed out separately.

Agnello alla Montagniola

Serves 10

for the meat

1.4kg (3lb) shoulder or leg of lamb, trimmed and cut into 2.5cm (1in) pieces
a dash of white wine vinegar
water

for the sauce

3 tablespoons Italian olive oil
3 leaves fresh sage
1 sprig rosemary
1 bayleaf
2-3 cloves garlic to taste, crushed (skin on)
1 wine glass red wine
1/2 onion, peeled and very finely chopped
10 ripe tomatoes, peeled, deseeded and chopped
salt to taste and freshly ground black pepper
25ml (1fl oz) brandy
1-2 tablespoons parsley, finely chopped

This traditional Italian dish, from the central region of Abruzzo is a popular Sunday meal for the family and is also often served at Easter time and at christenings. Gio told me that it is said – beware the troublesome lamb in the shepherd's mountain flock – he's the one who tries the shepherd's patience once too often and goes into the pot!

1 For the preparation before cooking the dish, first rinse the lamb and pat dry with kitchen paper. Put into a large pan, add the vinegar, cover with cold water and bring up to simmering point on a moderate flame. Cook for about five minutes, remove from the heat, cool and skim the fat from the surface of the cooking liquid. Strain the meat through a large sieve and set aside.

2 When you are ready to cook, heat up two tablespoons of olive oil in a large heavy-based frying pan on a moderate flame. Add the meat and stir and fry until the lamb takes on some colour, adding the sage, rosemary, bay leaf and whole crushed garlic – this takes about five minutes' cooking time.

3 Pour in the red wine, bring up to simmering point, turn down the flame, cover the pan and continue cooking for 15 minutes, stirring from time to time.

4 Meanwhile heat up the remaining one tablespoon of olive oil in a large heavy-based pan on a low to moderate flame, add the onion and fry gently until the onion is soft. Add the tomatoes and continue cooking for a few minutes.

5 Remove the whole herbs and garlic cloves from the simmering lamb and tip all the meat and juices into the pan of tomatoes – make sure you scrape all the meaty juices from the bottom of the pan.

6 Top up the pan with cold water to just cover, season with salt and pepper, add one tablespoon of chopped parsley, bring to simmering point, turn down the flame somewhat and cook gently for about one hour or until the meat is tender and the cooking liquid has reduced to produce a moist, creamy textured dish. Check for taste and adjust seasoning. Throw in the brandy, shake the pan to cook it through, flavour and amalgamate.

7 To serve, turn the Agnello alla Montagniola into a large warmed serving dish, sprinkle with parsley and serve immediately with roasted potatoes and a crisp green salad.

Filleti di Spigola alla Siciliana

Serves 2–4

2 fillets of spigola (sea bass)
1–2 tablespoons seasoned flour
1 tablespoon olive oil
½ glass vino bianco (dry white wine)
2 large ripe tomatoes, peeled, deseeded and diced
50g (2oz) unsalted butter, chilled and diced
4–5 black olives, pitted and sliced
1 teaspoon capers, drained

to finish

chopped parsley
wedges of lemon

Sea bass is another champion fish. Firm flesh, almost free of bones and a fabulous flavour, it's always best cooked simply with the minimum of fuss. It must be really fresh and ask your fishmonger to scale, gut and fillet it for you.

1 First, slice the tomatoes in half, squeeze out the pips and dice the flesh. Set aside.

2 Rinse the fillets of fish and pat dry with kitchen paper. Depending on their size and how many people you are serving, cut and trim the fillets accordingly for two to four servings. Coat very lightly in the seasoned flour.

3 Heat up the olive oil in a medium-sized heavy-based frying pan on a moderate flame. When the oil is hot put the fillets in the pan and fry for about one minute. Use one or two perforated spatulas to turn them carefully and fry for one more minute, or until the fish is just cooked – the cooking time will depend upon the thickness of the fillets but do not overcook them. Use the spatulas to transfer the fillets to a warmed serving platter, cover, set aside and keep warm.

4 Pour the wine into the pan, scraping up the fishy bits from the base of the pan on the moderate heat, then add the diced tomatoes and stir. Swiftly add the diced butter, olives and capers and stir to amalgamate and heat through – about thirty seconds.

5 Pour the pan juices over the spigola, garnish with chopped parsley and take immediately to the table to serve. Have a dish of lemon wedges to hand.

Fragole Giovanni

Serves 4

350g (12oz) strawberries, hulled,
  rinsed and chopped
300ml (½pint) double cream
50g (2oz) caster sugar
2 measures of vodka

1 Drain the washed, chopped strawberries. Divide them into four glass serving dishes and chill in the refrigerator.

2 Put the cream into a mixing bowl and whisk until it thickens, whisk in the sugar to incorporate, then add the vodka. Heap on to the chilled strawberries and serve straight away.

Gelato al Forno

Serves 4

110g (4oz) best quality dark
  chocolate
2 egg whites
25g (1oz) icing sugar
75g (3oz) ricotta cheese
3 tablespoons double cream
2 scoops of best quality dairy cream
  vanilla ice-cream

to finish the dish
a little icing sugar

A very special, seriously wicked dessert. The chocolate base can be prepared ahead of time, but the final dish must be prepared and cooked immediately prior to serving.

1 Preset the oven to 190°C/375°F/gas mark 5.

2 To melt the chocolate, put the pieces into a heat proof bowl over a pan of gently simmering water.

3 Pour the melted chocolate on to an oven proof plate, spreading it to form a circle and leave it to cool.

4 Put the room-temperature egg whites into a very clean and dry bowl (copper for best results), and whisk with the icing sugar until stiff and the mixture forms short peaks. Fold in the ricotta and the double cream.

5 Heap two scoops of ice-cream onto the cooled chocolate base and quickly coat with meringue. Put into the pre-heated oven for one minute only. Sprinkle with icing sugar and serve immediately.

Index